GOD OF THE VALLEY

Published by
The Bible Reading Fellowship
First Floor, Elsfield Hall
15–17 Elsfield Way, Oxford OX2 8FG

ISBN 1 84101 338 2
First published 2003
10 9 8 7 6 5 4 3 2 1 0

Acknowledgments
Unless otherwise stated, scripture quotations are taken from the Good
News Bible published by The Bible Societies/HarperCollins Publishers
Ltd, UK © American Bible Society 1966, 1971, 1976, 1992.

Scripture quotations from the Revised Standard Version of the Bible,
published by HarperCollins Publishers, are copyright © 1946, 1952,
1971 by the Division of Christian Education of the National Council of
the Churches of Christ in the USA, and are used by permission. All
rights reserved.

A catalogue record for this book is available from the British Library

Printed and bound in Great Britain by
Bookmarque, Croydon

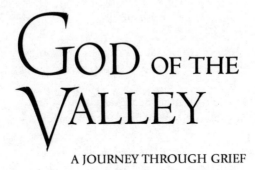

GOD OF THE VALLEY

A JOURNEY THROUGH GRIEF

STEVE GRIFFITHS

For Rebekah—
my inspiration and guide on the journey

For my parents and for Kathy and Mike—
who have constantly given sacrificial support

For Jo, Scott and Lee—
who have brought me comfort and hope for the future

For Clare and Jackie—
two great saints who inspired me more than they could ever
have known

CONTENTS

It is not the critic who counts;
not the man who points out where the strong man stumbled
or where the doer of deeds could have done better.
The credit belongs to the man who is actually in the arena;
whose face is marred by dust and sweat and blood;
who strives valiantly,
who errs and comes short again and again;
who knows the great enthusiasms;
who, at the best, knows the triumph of high achievement;
and who, at the worst, if he fails,
at least fails while daring greatly,
so that his place shall never be with those cold and timid souls
who know neither victory nor defeat.

THEODORE ROOSEVELT

FOREWORD

Death is commonplace. It happens once in every lifetime. Therefore, bereavement is also commonplace. Every friendship, every marriage, every parent–child relationship must inevitably end one day. As one who has quite recently experienced the loss of a partner, companion and friend of forty years, I know the sharp pain of separation and the continuing pain of loss—what Steve Griffiths calls 'the grinding and rubbing process' of sorrow. I also know that I share that experience with millions and millions of others. For each of us there is no shortage of advice and many, many stories to compare with our own.

There are plenty of books that relate those stories but, to be frank, I have not been anxious to read most of them. For one thing, when the cup of sorrow is full, there is nothing to gain by pouring yet more suffering—someone else's—into it. For another, those books that tell the story vividly are altogether too painful, and those that concern the loss of young lives or the tearing apart of new love simply raw tragedy. Sometimes such books, I have felt, raise questions but offer no answers. We are invited to weep, but without hope.

Steve Griffiths' book is different, which is why I am more than happy to write this foreword. He relates a sad story of loss, it is true, but—rather like C.S. Lewis in *A Grief Observed*—he also sets out to put the experience into a faith perspective. This is a book by a Christian about the Christian experience of bereavement. More than that, he has dried his eyes enough to be the teacher and pastor that he is, and to explore, with simplicity and sympathy, the teaching of the Bible about this universal sorrow. This is truth through story, through poetry, through the experience of God's people down the ages. It shows us how the Bible can speak with peculiar power and relevance to our own experience of personal loss. And it is full of Christian hope. In the end, it focuses on the call of the risen Jesus— there are 'sheep to be fed', a life to be lived. There is life after bereavement: the valley of the shadow offers a way ahead.

David Winter

A STORY OF PAIN

I steered into my driveway and brought the car to a halt. Grabbing my briefcase, I got out eagerly and made my way to the front door. I remember that I was whistling. Life was good. I had been ordained less than three months, our first daughter, Rebekah, was four months old and we were beginning to settle down in our new parish environment. That night, we were due out to dinner with the local Methodist Superintendent and his wife. He was a very down-to-earth guy and it would be a fun evening.

I turned the key in the door, shouted a 'Hello' to my wife, Clare, and took my coat off in the hall. The house was quiet and I sensed straight away that something was wrong. I walked into the front room. It was shrouded in darkness, the lights off, the curtains drawn. Rebekah was sleeping peacefully in her pram. Clare was lying on the sofa, motionless and clutching her head. In a barely audible voice, she told me that she had the most dreadful migraine, unlike anything else she had ever experienced. I managed to get her up the stairs and into bed. I cancelled dinner with a heavy heart, inwardly annoyed that Clare should have to be ill on this day of all days. I regret that selfishness now, of course.

The next day, Clare had no sign of a migraine. Nevertheless, she was unusually quiet and, when pushed, told me that she 'just didn't feel right'. Post-natal stuff, we thought. And then, within a week, everything began to change. Clare started having minor seizures, *petit-mal* epileptic fits and absences—small at first, but increasingly powerful and frequent. Within a few weeks, she was experiencing fifteen such episodes a day. We went to the doctor but he was convinced that it was post-natal depression. He prescribed Valium. When we got outside the surgery, Clare ripped up the prescription and burst into tears. 'Can't he see that I'm dying?' she cried. I chastised her for being so melodramatic. I regret that selfishness now, of course.

I will never forget New Year's Eve 1993. We watched TV together and went to bed. About 2.00 in the morning, Clare started making the weirdest noise I had ever heard. I switched the light on and, to my horror, saw her foaming at the mouth, body jerking and eyes rolling. I thought she was choking. I put my fingers into her mouth to free her tongue but she clamped her jaw shut. My fingers were trapped and I screamed in pain. I realized that Clare was having a *grand-mal* seizure—I had never witnessed anyone having an epileptic fit before and I was scared. Eventually, the fit subsided, I was able to make Clare comfortable and I phoned for an ambulance. She was admitted to hospital where the doctors ran various checks on her. Clare was booked for a brain scan on 13 February.

I remember the scan. I remember the fear in Clare's eyes as she went into the MRI tunnel. I remember the staff talking together in the adjacent room. I remember one of them coming over to me and asking in a casual but forced voice, 'When is Clare next due to see her doctor?' I remember sensing that all was far from well and I remember the dull ache in my stomach that I felt for the first time at that moment—a dull ache that was to become my constant companion. I remember them offering to seek out a doctor straight away.

The doctor was excellent. I don't remember the words he used but I do remember the tie he was wearing. Strange, isn't it? I do remember him describing the nature of Clare's brain tumour and I remember him showing us the scan, pointing out the enormous shadow that took up nearly one-quarter of Clare's brain area. I don't remember my response, but I remember Clare saying, 'I'm going to die, aren't I?' I remember the glazed expression in the doctor's eyes as he said, 'Most probably, yes. I'm so sorry.' I remember Clare saying, 'Oh, poor Rebekah!' and I remember bursting into tears. The rest is a blur.

The next few weeks were a frantic round of medical

appointments. Offers of this palliative care and that palliative care, more words, words, words. Lots of words but no hope. Eventually, we contacted a medical friend in London and asked if he knew anyone who could give a second opinion. His colleague was Mr Henry Marsh, a quite brilliant neurosurgeon. A phone call later and we were on our way to London to meet this man. He took a look at the scans and offered to operate immediately, under local anaesthetic, to try out a new technique he was working on. The operation took place on 15 March. All went well until the final stages when Clare had a seizure and a minor stroke. The operation had to be concluded at haste and a small area of tumour was left in the brain.

Clare's recovery was painfully slow: she could not talk or walk or eat properly for nearly two weeks. Eventually, she was well enough to leave hospital. The next twelve months were the toughest period of our lives. Clare was battling against the impact of a stroke—her right side was all but useless. She was suffering constant headaches and regular epileptic fits. Her speech was impaired. She could no longer drive, of course, and she was also unable to pursue her artistic hobbies—painting, sewing, dress-making and the like. She could not walk properly, she could not bath herself, she could not undertake even the most basic of tasks without help. Most painful of all, she could not hold Rebekah safely without help. We were living far from our family and I was trying to look after her, raise our young daughter, continue my PhD studies and minister within the parish. Looking back now, I realize that God gave us both strength in an impossible situation.

The next four years were a regular round of scans and medical check-ups. Clare's health improved but she still suffered from periodic fits and her right side was never strong again. We had weeks and months when we could live happily together as a normal family; we had weeks and months when our experiences were far from normal; and always hanging over us, like the Sword of Damocles, was that little tumour in Clare's brain that we knew would one day take her life. We were living on borrowed time.

How ironic, then, to come home in 1997 to find my sister, Jackie, sitting in my front room. Like Clare, she was 33 and she had two daughters, aged four and three. We made a coffee and she told me that she had been diagnosed with breast cancer. We cried together and we prayed together. Her treatment was radical— mastectomy, radiotherapy and chemotherapy. For a short while, Jackie was in remission, but just before Christmas 1998, it was discovered that she too had developed secondary cancer in the brain. Once more we turned to Henry Marsh, who operated. Sadly, there was less success this time. Jackie deteriorated rapidly as the cancer spread throughout her body. She was dead by May.

I could scarcely take it in. Emotionally, I had been preparing myself for the death of my wife. Now it was my only sibling who had gone. In addition, my friend Dave died during the same period, again from a brain disorder arising from a freak epileptic seizure. He was 34. In the autumn, my grandad and Clare's grandmother died. It was all too much to take and yet, somehow, God gave me the strength to perform their funerals and for us to get through this dark time.

It may have been the shock of so much grief in such a short period of time that triggered Clare's relapse. Certainly, the pain of watching my sister die of the same illness that would eventually take her life had profoundly affected her. We had Christmas 2000 together but we knew it would be our last. We bought a camcorder to record our celebrations. With a heavy heart, I went to teach in India in February but was soon recalled when Clare collapsed. More surgery under Henry Marsh; more radiotherapy; 34 tablets a day that still could not control the epilepsy or the migraines. By April, Clare could not put a sentence of coherent speech together. She could not remember my name or Rebekah's. She had frequent mood swings. Her mobility worsened daily and she fell regularly. Increasingly, she spent her days asleep. The rest is too painful to mention here.

Clare died in July. She was 36. I was 34. Rebekah was 8.

This book is written out of my experience of grief—not just the deaths of Clare and Jackie and Dave and our grandparents, but also out of the privilege of having sat with dozens of families as we have prepared for funerals together, and out of the immense privilege of having sat with a number of others as they have died. There is a sense in which I have little to offer anyone on this subject. I am not a trained bereavement counsellor and I know little of the theory behind the bereavement process. I am also deeply aware that each journey into and through grief is profoundly unique and that comparisons cannot be drawn. However, I am more aware still of the fact that God has strengthened me in the valley of the shadow of death and that I have found great comfort in him and his word to me. I am not qualified to write a book on bereavement, but I am qualified, as a child of God, to share with you my thoughts on a number of biblical passages that have sustained me throughout the years.

Some of the passages may be familiar to those of us working through grief. Others may be less familiar. I have tried to keep each chapter fairly short—I know that grief has an impact on one's ability to concentrate for any period of time. Longer pieces would be counter-productive. However, my hope is that, as I interweave aspects of my journey with the Bible passages that have meant the most to me, so you may be drawn closer to the living God who stands with us in our darkest hours—the God who himself has experienced the shadow of death—the God of the Valley.

CHAPTER ONE

YOU MAY NOT WANT
TO HEAR THIS

Job and Ecclesiastes

*'I was born with nothing, and I will die with nothing. The Lord gave,
and now he has taken away. May his name be praised!'*
JOB 1:21

This book begins with the tough question, the toughest question
of all, the question we all ask: 'Why?' There is no point avoiding
that question in a book like this. There's no point waiting until a
later chapter to discuss it. This is the big one—the question in the
face of which so many of us either stand or fall. In dealing with it,
I want to consider just one part of scripture that seems to address
the issue with real clarity—the Wisdom literature in the Old Testament. The Wisdom literature encompasses a whole range of books
—Job, Ecclesiastes, Song of Songs, Psalms, Proverbs—and parts of
other books, like Daniel. All of these books ask profound questions
about the human experience of suffering and loss in the most direct
and pragmatic ways. It is in the Wisdom literature that we find the
question 'Why?' expressed most coherently. A warning to you at
the very outset, however: in thinking about this question, you may
not want to hear the answer.

THE CLOUD OF UNKNOWING

One of the greatest Christian books ever written is called *The Cloud of Unknowing*. It was written in the 14th century. No one knows who the author was—maybe a country parson in the East Midlands, England—but it doesn't matter who wrote it. He had some excellent things to say about our relationship with God and the spiritual journey we are on. The book is about developing a prayer life and a spirituality that is able to function in the most difficult times of life as well as when everything is going well. The author describes it like this:

When you first begin [the spiritual exercise], you find only darkness, and as it were a cloud of unknowing. You don't know what this means except that in your will you feel a simple steadfast intention reaching out towards God. Do what you will, this darkness and this cloud remain between you and God, and stop you, both from seeing him in the clear light of rational understanding, and from experiencing his loving sweetness in your affection. Reconcile yourself to wait in this darkness as long as is necessary, but still go on longing after him whom you love. For if you are to feel him or to see him in this life, it must always be in this cloud, in this darkness.[1]

As the author of *The Cloud of Unknowing* attempts to describe our relationship with God, there is a sense in which he captures the atmosphere of much of the Wisdom writers' attitude to the problem of suffering—what is known as 'theodicy'. We struggle to understand the rightness of the actions of God when we suffer loss or grief. We are in a place of utter darkness—a cloud of unknowing. Yet it is *in* that darkness that the Wisdom writers exhort us to find our rest. Indeed, it is precisely that darkness, that state of unknowing, which reveals the true nature of God in relationship to our suffering. You may not want to hear this, but the answer to the problem of theodicy, according to the Wisdom writers, is that there is no answer available, and that must be sufficient for us in itself. There's no point asking the question 'Why?' because the answer will never be known. However, far from being a negative response, this attitude actually forms the basis for joy and hope. The example of the Wisdom writers, and the experience of so many individuals, is that as the irony of suffering is understood and accepted, so we are able to accept with renewed clarity the irony of grace. Life is perceived from a new perspective—a perspective that is founded upon an acceptance of our true nature in relation to the Sovereign God. So let's make the journey with the Wisdom writers in this, focusing especially on the book of Ecclesiastes and the book of Job.

DEFENDING GOD

Theodicy is actually about more than the problem of suffering or evil in the world. It is about defending God in the light of suffering and evil. As if God needs defending by us! Nevertheless, when we are grieving, this is the question we ask: how can suffering and evil in the world be reconciled with the existence of a God who is supposed to be unlimited in terms of both power and love? Theodicy, then, is an attempt to return a verdict of 'not guilty' on God when we are faced with the reality of evil and suffering.

When we read the Wisdom literature, however, we see that the writers make little or no attempt to solve the problem of theodicy. They do not try to justify God in the light of personal suffering. Instead, they are more concerned to bring the reader to a point whereby the problems faced may be considered in a godly fashion rather than one driven purely by emotion. The issue of suffering is considered in a wider context than theodicy alone. God stands in the dock, not on his own, but with humanity by his side. Job, for example, is anxious to prove himself 'not guilty' as well. But we are jumping the gun a bit here.

In his book *Israel's Praise*, Walter Brueggemann wrote, 'All true theology begins in pain... It is the reality of concrete pain known in the specificity of a person or a community which is the locus of serious faith.'[2] What Brueggemann is suggesting is that the experience of pain actually opens the door to life—and life in abundance. Our experiences of suffering and grief can prove to be the way in which we grow with God and come to know both him and ourselves better. Pain is to be embraced, not denied; utilized, not shunned. Our experience of pain provides the foundation for godly living. As Bruggemann says, 'Hope lives in and becomes operative only in the hurt.'[3] This is an attitude that we find in the Wisdom literature. With regard to theodicy, there are four common themes that run through this part of scripture: the sovereignty of God, an understanding of the nature of humanity in relation to the sovereign God, the irony of indiscriminate suffering and an understanding of the irony of grace. We will examine each of these four ideas in turn.

THE SOVEREIGNTY OF GOD

In many churches today, it is increasingly uncommon to make the sovereignty of God a starting point, especially when faced with the issues of suffering and grief. I was told of one church recently where a teenage girl was diagnosed with cancer. Quite rightly, the congregation dedicated many hours to praying for her healing. Her condition deteriorated rapidly but still the congregation prayed in faith, claiming the healing promises of scripture for her. Sadly, the girl died and the congregation have found it very hard to accept that this should have happened. On a weekly basis, four members of the church stand over her grave and pray for her resurrection. They have vowed not to give up until she is brought back to life.

The sovereignty of God is a given absolute in the Wisdom literature. God is sovereign, full stop. Everything else needs to be considered in the light of that awesome truth. In Ecclesiastes 9:1 we read that 'God controls the actions of wise and righteous people'. Likewise in Job, the sovereignty of God shines through in many of the speeches: 'God is so wise and powerful; no one can stand up against him' (Job 9:4). In Proverbs 3:19, we are reminded of the sovereign God who 'created the earth by his wisdom; by his knowledge he set the sky in place'. This is the starting point for the Wisdom writers in understanding God and their own experiences of him. Thus their experiences of suffering and grief must be put into that context. We serve a sovereign God who is so far above us and so awesome and majestic and powerful that, ultimately, his ways cannot be questioned, let alone challenged. For that reason, the idea of theodicy—attempting to declare God 'not guilty' in the light of our bitter experiences—is a nonsense. For the Wisdom writers, there is no point in trying to solve the problem of suffering or suppress the impact of suffering. Rather, the challenge is to find meaning of life within the pain and to learn how to use that pain creatively in a relationship with God.

CREATURES BEFORE THE CREATOR

The flip-side of the coin, then, is to understand the nature of our humanity in the context of the sovereignty of God. The theologian Karl Barth wrote:

At the very points where [man] seems to speak most strongly, say in Job, or Ecclesiastes… he is in fact most securely bound to that relationship, to that absolutely real relationship of super- and sub-ordination, which precedes all the expressions and experiences of his life with God, and which withdraws only in appearance, but is never completely obscured.[4]

So, in Job 1:21, the main character can say, 'I was born with nothing, and I will die with nothing. The Lord gave, and now he has taken away. May his name be praised!' This is not a statement of mock humility. Nor is it a sign that Job had given up all hope. Instead, Job recognized that God is sovereign and that he, as a mere mortal, existed as a subordinate within that relationship. The plain truth is that God owed Job nothing. The harsh reality is that God owes us nothing. The Lord gives and the Lord takes away. Blessed is the name of the Lord. To comprehend and survive our own bitter experience of grief, we must never lose sight of the fact that we are mere creatures before an awesome Creator. The writer of Ecclesiastes reminds us, 'As you do not know how the spirit comes to the bones in the womb of a woman with child, so you do not know the work of God who makes everything' (Ecclesiastes 11:5, RSV).

So there is a real paradox at work in the Wisdom literature. God is recognized as sovereign and, as such, his ways are beyond questioning. Yet there is a sense in which human beings still feel the need to question. When we suffer grief and loss, we question the unquestionable. We know that our questioning is illogical; we know that we will never be given an answer; but we question all the same.

Some companions on our journey through suffering tried to convince us that questioning God was wrong. Clare and I were, on a number of occasions, told that we should just sit under the sovereignty of God and accept our lot. That was most unhelpful because the pain of Clare's terminal illness was now compounded by a sense of guilt that we were behaving in an unChristian way. Not only are these types of comment unhelpful, however, they are also ungodly. What is most interesting to me when reading the story of Job is that he is allowed to ask the question 'Why?' over and over again before God answers him. Throughout Job's speeches, the alternation between affirming the sovereignty of God and the demand for God to justify himself is highly significant. In chapter 9:10, for example, Job extols the nature of God 'who does great things beyond understanding, and marvellous things without number' (RSV). Yet in chapter 10:3, he questions God thus: 'Is it right for you to be so cruel? To despise what you yourself have made? And then to smile on the schemes of wicked people?' Oscillating between these two approaches is a common experience for all of us who have suffered grief. One hour, we sit quietly under the sovereign authority of God. The next hour, we shout out in anger for him to explain what on earth is going on. How can we justify that?

It seems to me that what Job is actually doing is not questioning the sovereignty of God at all. Deep in his heart, he knows that God is beyond all knowing. He fully respects the authority of God. In asking the question 'Why?' what Job is actually doing is trying to affirm his own humanity, his own sense of worth. Job wants to be reassured that even though he is a creature, he has some sense of worth in the eyes of God. He needs to know that he is valuable. When God finally appears and speaks with Job in 38:1—41:34, it is striking that he does not reveal anything that Job had not already verbalized. All God does is to reaffirm his own sovereignty. Yet it has been an important process for Job to question God and work through the issue of his own creaturely humanity so that, when God finally does appear, he is not crushed. Job has asked the question 'Why?' He has recognized the sovereignty of God. He has understood that he is nothing more than a creature of God. He has become convinced that, even as a creature, he is valuable and has worth. He has found some sense of peace in his cloud of unknowing. And then God appears to him.

THE IRONY OF INDISCRIMINATE SUFFERING

That, then, is the context in which we must grapple with our own bitter experience of grief and suffering. But where do we go from there? The next stage, according to the Wisdom literature, is to recognize and accept the irony of indiscriminate suffering. Note that I do not say that indiscriminate suffering is unjust. To say that would be to create a condition on the sovereign God. Rather, indiscriminate suffering is ironic.

During the first few months after Clare's diagnosis, we were both greatly strengthened by the public ministry of the entertainer Roy Castle. He had been diagnosed with lung cancer despite the fact that he had never smoked. His illness, it seemed, had developed through passive smoking while working in various clubs around the country. Roy Castle was a Christian and spoke with great honesty and clarity about his illness and his faith. A turning point for Clare and me came when watching him interviewed on breakfast TV. The interviewer asked him if he had ever asked the question, 'Why me?' I don't remember exactly how he answered but the gist of it was that, more often than not, he asked, 'Why not me?'

That was a profound moment of revelation for us and his example was one that we consciously decided to develop for ourselves. We realized that the truth of the matter is quite simple. People develop brain tumours. People develop cancer. People die young. That's life. There is no rhyme or reason to it. Terminal illness is completely indiscriminate as to whom it affects. Why should any one of us expect to be immune from this harsh reality? So, the question for Clare and me was not so much 'Why me?' as 'Why not me?'

The Wisdom writers were profoundly aware that there is a real irony about the way in which suffering and grief are so indiscriminate. The entire emphasis of Job's argument is a diatribe on this reality—he knew that he was a godly man and yet he had not been protected from terrible loss. In Ecclesiastes 8:14, we read this understanding of the way things are: 'Look at what happens in the world: sometimes the righteous get the punishment of the wicked, and the wicked get the reward of the righteous. I say it is useless.' Both writers came to the same understanding in different ways. Job had to wrestle in prayer and go through an extraordinary period of mental anguish. The writer of Ecclesiastes took time out to reflect on his philosophy of life. Both methods of reaching the same conclusion are equally valid. We all respond differently in times of trial. But to come to terms with the reality of the irony of indiscriminate suffering was a vital stage for both writers in their relationship with God. So we too need to recognize objectively that life can sometimes just be very, very cruel. It is an objective recognition that is required. If we are to learn how to rest in the cloud of unknowing, we must stop boxing shadows. In *The Way of Wisdom*, R. Scott wrote, 'What God is in himself remains mysterious. What he expects of men is unknown. Man can only use his powers of observation, seek understanding through reflection, and acquiesce in what cannot be altered.'[5] That is not giving up hope. That is facing reality.

THE IRONY OF GRACE

If the Wisdom writers were to leave the problem of theodicy at that point, they could rightly be accused, as has so often been the case, of holding to a pessimistic worldview. However, there is one final development that the Wisdom writers make in order to present an objective understanding of suffering and grief—namely that as we begin to accept indiscriminate suffering as ironic, so it becomes clear that existence in general—and God's grace in particular—is ironic too. When this final stage of understanding is reached, the problem of suffering and grief can be viewed in a new and proper perspective in the context of a created order of which humanity is just one part. In examining this, we can look at three examples— Ecclesiastes, Job and also some Wisdom writing in the book of Daniel.

Punctuating the admittedly often downbeat writings in Ecclesiastes, there are exhortations to make the most of life—enjoy yourself, make merry, enjoy your youth, live life to the full. There seems to be a paradox here. The writer constantly says that all is vanity, fruitless, without result—the Hebrew word is *hebel*. All is *hebel*. Seemingly, this is a view of hopelessness. But let's just reflect on exactly what the writer considers to be *hebel*. In 1:14, he refers to 'everything that is done under the sun' (RSV). In 2:11, it is hard work and personal effort that is *hebel*, while, at the beginning of that chapter, the writer suggests that the pursuit of happiness is a waste of time. In 2:13–15, the pursuit of wisdom is reckoned to be *hebel*. It seems that the writer is fully aware of the irony of life. It doesn't matter how hard we work or what we do to gain wisdom and happiness, we can never achieve these things. Life, by its very nature, is hallmarked by incongruity and irony. This is an important point for those of us working through the process of grief because, once we come to recognize that the whole of life is incongruous and ironic, we are able to gain a more realistic perspective. It is not just the experience of indiscriminate suffering that is ironic. The whole of life is like that too!

That understanding of the irony of existence is found in the well-known story of Shadrach, Meshach and Abednego in Daniel 3. When faced with a painful execution in the furnace, hear what they say to King Nebuchadnezzar: 'Your Majesty, we will not try to defend ourselves. If the God whom we serve is able to save us from the blazing furnace and from your power, then he will. But even if he doesn't, Your Majesty may be sure that we will not worship your god, and we will not bow down to the gold statue that you have set up' (3:16–18). By answering the king in that way, the three men fully accepted the irony of existence. For them, the issue of indiscriminate suffering and death, and the role of God within that, was swallowed up in a broader worldview: life and death are in the hands of the sovereign God whom they served. Whether they lived or whether they died, the irony lay in the fact that their very existence was in the hands of a being more powerful than they. Within the context of that sovereignty, they were prepared to accept the condition of their fate and they would find joy in whatever lay ahead.

Finally, the book of Job finishes with the main character and the reader left in no doubt about the irony of existence. 'I know, Lord, that you are all-powerful; that you can do everything you want... I am so very ignorant. I talked about things I did not understand, about marvels too great for me to know... So I am ashamed of all I have said and repent in dust and ashes' (42:2–3, 6). In the last five chapters of that book, the sheer power of the imagery portrayed in God's speech reveals the fact that creaturely existence is held in the palm of God's hand and that to live at all is a wonderful act of grace on behalf of the sovereign Lord. Since the gift of life is such an amazing and undeserved act of grace, who are we to complain when that gift of life is taken from us? We don't deserve God's grace—it is ironic. The irony of indiscriminate suffering must be viewed within that context.

THE FRAMEWORK

It is entirely natural, when we suffer tragedy and loss, to ask the question 'Why?' It is entirely natural to want God to explain himself to us, to justify his inactivity in not intervening in the way that we might expect. Is God to be declared 'guilty' or 'not guilty'? The Wisdom writers do not try to solve this problem. What they do succeed in doing, however, is to provide a framework within which the problem of theodicy can be considered. It is a framework that clarifies the sovereignty of God. It is a framework that acknowledges the position of creaturely humanity before the awesome Creator God. It is a framework that enables the reader to consider with honesty the reality of indiscriminate suffering, without losing sight of the irony of existence and the irony of undeserved grace. But most importantly, it is a framework that takes seriously the reality of pain. Rather than attempting to justify God by either ignoring that pain or decrying the nature of humanity, the writers use that pain as a base from which to consider the harsh reality of indiscriminate suffering. It is with brutal honesty that they conclude, by virtue of their silence, that there is no answer to the question 'Why?' But by approaching the question in the manner they do, they provide a framework in which each one of us may begin to learn how to rest in our own cloud of unknowing.

CHAPTER TWO

LOOK AFTER NUMBER ONE

1 Kings 19:1-9

Elijah got up, ate and drank, and the food gave him enough strength to walk forty days to Sinai, the holy mountain.
1 KINGS 19:8

RUN FOR YOUR LIFE

I was on a roll. I had never felt so good. I had been pursuing a concentrated training programme for the London Marathon for two months and was beginning to push myself beyond limits that I had previously only dreamt about. This particular afternoon, I had run for thirteen miles and was feeling like I could go on for ever. I was a long way from home, jogging along a country lane that I had not been down before. I had heard about 'the wall'—that physical and mental barrier that runners need to pass through, the other side of which exists a mental 'high' that gives a sense of invincibility. I had just broken through my 'wall'. My pace quickened, my breathing got easier and the burning of cramp was receding. Then disaster struck. My right leg gave way beneath me as my shin began to throb with pain. I collapsed in agony by the side of the road and rested there for a while. Eventually, I got to my feet and tried to run on but only made it another twenty yards. With a heavy heart, I admitted defeat and had to face the prospect of a long, slow and painful thirteen-mile walk back home. That afternoon marked the end of my Marathon hopes: I had shin splints and could not run on tarmac without causing the problem again. I was upset, of course, but still had other activities to keep me fit. I was swimming four miles a week and going to the gym three times a week. To be sure, I would miss my runs but I could still stay fit without them.

Keeping fit had become very important to me. Perhaps there was a subconscious element about needing to control something. Clare was recovering well from her first bout of brain surgery but life was still extremely difficult for us both. I was looking after her during the day and, at night, she was having regular epileptic fits. Rebekah was less than a year old and I was carrying a great deal of the weight of parenthood. I had begun a new ministry and was studying for a PhD at the same time. While I gave the outward impression of coping well, emotionally I was sinking fast. I was tired, confused, disorientated, overworked and overstressed. I needed some release, both physically and emotionally, and my fitness routine was proving a good way of bringing some order into my life.

During the early years of Clare's remission, I managed to stay reasonably fit. After a while, however, it became impossible to continue my routine. Clare's epilepsy became less predictable and I was increasingly concerned that she would have a fit while I was out. Her right side became weaker as time went by and she was less able to undertake basic tasks such as opening cans, holding a kettle, getting in and out of the bath and so on. Additionally, there were times when I was worried about Clare's ability to look after Rebekah. Most of the time, she could cope very well indeed. Occasionally, however, I could tell from her disposition when an epileptic fit was coming on and I would not want to leave Rebekah in her care at those times.

Gradually, I began to put on weight. Nothing drastic—just enough for my closest friends to begin making casual jokes at my expense. Because I was not spending so much time exercising, I was working increasingly long hours and was becoming more tired and stressed. I was a smoker in those days, too, and was feeling increasingly ill with chest pains. I developed a bad skin condition on my hands that caused no small social embarrassment for me. In the year prior to Clare's death, her condition deteriorated considerably and I found it almost impossible to leave her for any length of time on her own. Carrying almost all the burden of running a home, caring for a sick wife, bringing up a young daughter as well as working full time took an increasingly heavy toll on my health. I was absolutely exhausted, both physically and mentally. Due to time and energy constraints, it was often easier to rely on takeaways rather than cooking a healthy meal.

I was three-and-a-half stone overweight when Clare died. My skin condition was so bad that I often had my hands bandaged. The levels of stress in my life were higher than anything I had ever experienced before. I was exhausted beyond all comprehension and was very close to breaking point. I remember standing in front of a mirror two weeks after Clare's funeral. I no longer recognized the tired, fat old man whose haunted expression stared back at me. I cried. With tears rolling down my cheeks, I realized that if I did not do something drastic to redeem the situation, Rebekah may well soon be an orphan.

LEARNING FROM SEATTLE

One of my favourite films is *Sleepless in Seattle* with Tom Hanks and Meg Ryan. A real weepy, it is the story of a young widower called Sam who finds love again with a stranger through a series of occurrences strategically masterminded and arranged by his young son, Jonah. Initially, Jonah secretly telephones a radio chat show and asks the guest doctor to help find a new partner for his father. Eventually, Sam is encouraged to speak on the live phone-in show about the impact of grief and bereavement. Asked how he will cope, he says, 'I'm going to get out of bed every morning, breathe in and out all day long, and then after a while I won't have to remind myself to get out of bed in the morning and breathe in and out.'

Perhaps the greatest surprise for me in the aftermath of losing Clare was just how exhausting grief can be. I was completely unprepared for the impact of the overwhelming tiredness I felt. I am also convinced that this is one aspect of grief that is wholly misunderstood by those who have never experienced the anguish of losing someone close to them. This exhaustion had four primary ramifications for my day-to-day activities.

First, my sleep patterns became erratic in the extreme. I simply could not face going to bed alone so I would either lie there listening to the radio all night or else sleep on the sofa downstairs. I soon managed to get by on just three or four hours' sleep a night. I would watch TV into the small hours and would be doing the housework or some academic research as the sun rose.

Second, the exhaustion of grief resulted in a lack of energy for even the most basic of tasks. Work-related activities that would previously have taken an hour of my time now filled an entire day. My levels of concentration became so low that I would be able to spend only five or ten minutes at a particular assignment before wandering off to make yet another cup of coffee or switching on daytime TV. My short-term memory became seriously deficient and so I was constantly having to recover the details of schedules and work responsibilities or else apologize profusely to those who had been let down by my failure to remember appointments and arrangements.

Third, I lacked energy and motivation in contacting friends and family. Even the shortest of conversations left me exhausted and depressed. Without a partner, I no longer had the luxury of 'dipping in and out' of group conversations. I now had to constantly assess information and think what to say next. I was tired of having to tell people over and over again in a single day how I was getting on. Each person was sensitive enough to phone or visit for only five or ten minutes but they were unaware of being just one of perhaps twenty inquirers that day. I valued these people and was deeply touched by their concern, but by the end of the day I often felt mentally and emotionally raped by constantly having to bare my soul and expose my inner anguish with such regularity and intensity. Eventually, it became easier just to say, 'I'm fine, thanks', even though I was aware that this response led others to believe I was in some sort of denial.

Fourth, I found myself becoming extremely discerning about how to spend what little time and energy reserves I had within me. Never one for making much small talk with strangers, I now found myself not bothering to interact on a superficial level at all, and, uncharacteristically, not even caring if others thought of me as rude. I reasoned that I had little enough energy to survive the day and was not prepared to expend any on shallow personal inter-action. Additionally, I became increasingly annoyed by demands from others to engage in activities that I considered a waste of time. Attending meetings where people waffled became a dis-proportionate irritation to be endured. Phone calls that became 'chatty' exasperated me: 'Just give me the facts and leave me alone!' I screamed inside. Parishioners coming to me with trivial pastoral concerns maddened me: 'For goodness' sake, just deal with it! You call *that* a problem? It's nothing compared with what I've been through!' Having lost someone so precious at such a young age, I had become acutely aware that there is no time to waste in life. Every moment of my existence had to be lived to its full potential, and I was not about to allow anybody to rob me of whatever living I had left to do.

Most frightening of all was the stark realization that I was constantly on the edge of doing something very stupid. I do not mean suicide: the thought has never crossed my mind. For a long time after losing Clare, however, the anguish of grief bred a sub-conscious desire in me to 'self-destruct'. I was aware that just one little push would send me over the precipice. Sometimes I even wanted to be pushed. There were days when I would deliberately become antagonistic so that I could force an argument. Then, when I was alone that evening, I would have an excuse to feel sorry for myself and could seek comfort in a few glasses too many of Jack Daniels. Other times, I would subconsciously look for a reason to 'throw it all away'. Two or three times, I wrote my letter of resignation for the bishop, only to think better of it as I drove round to post it through his letterbox. I could no longer find any reason to carry on. I was tired. There seemed to be no end in sight. Like Sam in *Sleepless in Seattle*, I could not see beyond getting out of bed in the morning and reminding myself to take the next breath.

The first step towards receiving healing in grief was an intensely pragmatic one. I had to learn to look after Number One on a physical and emotional level before I could allow God to tend my spiritual wounds. This is not as selfish or 'unspiritual' as it may sound. Indeed, this pragmatic approach is an entirely biblical one, as the story of Elijah shows.

LOOK AFTER NUMBER ONE

1 Kings 19 is a well-known part of scripture, primarily for the description of the manifestation of God in 'the soft whisper of a voice' (v. 12). Important though this description of the activity of God is, the central theme of the chapter is not so much the theophany as Elijah's call to ministry. In terms reminiscent of so many Old Testament encounters between a prophet and God, Elijah is brought from self-doubt to a place of recommissioning in ministry. The story of that encounter with God is not our present concern, however. For our purposes, we are concerned only with the events that led up to that encounter, recorded in 1 Kings 19:1–9.

This part of Elijah's story must be set in the context of events that had occurred three days previously, recorded in chapter 18. Elijah had been on Mount Carmel, engaged in a colossal confrontation with the prophets of Baal. The reputation of the Lord God was at stake in this conflict. In the presence of hundreds of Israelites, 450 prophets of Baal and 400 prophets of the goddess Asherah, Elijah had performed a miracle that vindicated the existence and power of his God. After the miracle was complete, Elijah ordered the people of Israel to seize the prophets, take them to the River Kishon and execute them.

In that one triumphant moment, Elijah had discredited the powers of darkness, challenged the political and spiritual leaders of the nation and vindicated the power and authenticity of his own prophetic ministry. Queen Jezebel, the wife of the reigning King Ahab, was so infuriated and embarrassed by this incident that she sent a threatening message to Elijah: 'May the gods strike me dead if by this time tomorrow I don't do the same thing to you that you did to the prophets' (19:2). This threat from the queen was the incident that triggered Elijah's subsequent collapse.

In truth, Elijah was absolutely exhausted following his exertions on Mount Carmel. In that power encounter, he had given everything he possibly could. He was physically, emotionally and spiritually drained and, as a result, was unable to retain any perspective on the unfolding events. The threat that Jezebel had made threw Elijah into a state of overwhelming anxiety. We read in verse 3 that 'Elijah was afraid' and that his only thought was to escape by running away. Interestingly, it was not the reality of his present situation that caused Elijah to fall victim to fear and depression. Rather, it was fear of the future; fear of what torment might befall him at the hands of the queen. For a moment in time, Elijah ceased contemplation of the awesome, miraculous power of the God whom he served and became preoccupied instead with possible futures. The Hebrew in verse 3 that is translated 'Elijah was afraid' actually reads, 'Elijah sees how things are'. But the truth is that Elijah did not see how things were at all! Instead, he feared how things might turn out to be. As a result of stress and fear, Elijah had stopped discerning 'spiritually' and had begun merely reacting to the circumstances of life. Elijah was motivated to flee for his life because of his own assessment of the situation. He was not following a word from the Lord. Indeed, the path he followed stood in absolute contradiction to the will of God. Elijah fled to the furthest point south—Beersheba in Judah—but later, in verse 15, God would instruct him to go north again!

Verses 3 and 4 are deeply insightful, with so much information about the psychology of Elijah being revealed in the detail of the story. First, we are told, 'Leaving the servant there, Elijah walked a whole day into the wilderness.' There are two things to note here. In leaving his servant behind, Elijah was symbolically renouncing his prophetic ministry. His servant would have been his helper, freeing Elijah from domestic considerations to devote himself to his divine calling. By ridding himself of that helpmate, Elijah was acknowledging his belief that he no longer had a part to play in the purposes of God. Also, by leaving Beersheba and going into the wilderness, Elijah was effectively divorcing himself from the covenant people of God. His depression was such that he could not countenance living out an existence within the context of faith-relationships. There was no one to help him. There was no one who could possibly understand how he felt. Elijah just wanted to be left alone with God, to face whatever brief and empty future he might have in solitude.

There is something intensely poignant about the description of this lonely, tortured soul detailed in verse 4. The tree under which he sat was a 'broom-brush', the botanical name being *Retama roetam*, a tree growing to a height of over three metres. We can picture him sitting under this single tree in the wilderness seeking shade from the intense heat of the sun, utterly alone, contemplating death. There was nothing logical about his state of depression. After all, he had just experienced remarkable success on Mount Carmel and had witnessed the awesome power of his God. But the truth is that there is no logic in depression. Elijah was clearly disorientated and confused. In verse 3, we read that 'Elijah was afraid, and fled for his life.' In verse 4, he prays the exact opposite desire to God: 'Take away my life; I might as well be dead!' That oscillation between the innate desire to survive and the inclination to give up and die is not unusual for those suffering depression. For those afflicted by grief, this alternation between the determination to endure and the tendency to quit may happen not only on a day-by-day basis but even hourly.

Elijah was burnt out. Verse 5 starkly states, 'He lay down under the tree and fell asleep', but in that most natural response to fatigue began the process of his holistic restoration. God allowed him to slumber for a while before taking the initiative in sending an angel. It is interesting to note that, at this stage, the angel did not bring any spiritually profound message from the Lord. Rather, there was a gracious gentleness in his instruction: 'Wake up and eat' (v. 5). Elijah partook of the water and bread. Thereafter, the process of physical healing was allowed to continue as he went back to sleep.

Some time later, the angel of the Lord visited Elijah for a second time. There was a subtle difference to this visit, even though it was still manifestly compassionate. On this occasion, the angel woke Elijah and said, 'Get up and eat, or the journey will be too much for you' (v. 7). Here, there is a twofold emphasis on the beginning of a recommissioning to ministry. First, Elijah was encouraged to 'get up', rather than just 'wake up'. There was something more proactive required of him at this point. Second, there was mention of a journey upon which Elijah would soon be asked to embark. The emphasis was still on physical recuperation but there was the promise of a journey. Elijah had thought that his journey was finished in the wilderness but God had other ideas. The angel did not give any detail about where the journey would lead. He just gave hope that Elijah's present situation was not the end. Ironically, this withholding of information was, in itself, an act of grace. If the angel had given too much detail, it would no doubt have given Elijah more stress and he would have sunk into a deeper depression at the task that lay ahead. God was gently restoring him, physically and emotionally—in that order—before engaging him spiritually in active ministry once more.

In verse 8, we read of his response: 'Elijah got up, ate and drank, and the food gave him enough strength to walk forty days to Sinai, the holy mountain.' The fact that the journey lasted forty days and led to Mount Sinai is, of course, highly significant. Here, the expedition of Elijah is being likened to that of Moses and the people of Israel in Exodus. The challenge that lay ahead for him was simply this: would he be like Moses and receive the vision and calling of God on his life or would he become faithless and self-pitying like the Israelites? Upon arriving at Sinai, he went into a cave and spent the night there (v. 9). This period of rest marked the completion of this phase of Elijah's restoration. God had physically restored him through sleep, food and drink. God had emotionally restored him through the promise of a journey to a destination of the Lord's choosing. Having arrived at that destination, Elijah now became spiritually restored as he spent the night meditating and praying in a cave. Having been restored physically, emotionally and spiritually, Elijah was now ready to be met by God in a profoundly personal manner.

The detail of that meeting with God is not our primary concern here. Suffice it to note only that God was not to be found in the furious wind or the earthquake or the fire. Instead, God was to be found in 'the soft whisper of a voice' (v. 12). There are two things to note here. First, the experience of grief is often akin to that of wind, earthquake and fire in the soul. We feel tossed and blown around, victim to the elements. We feel torn asunder, with the very heart of our being ripped out from within us. We feel burnt by the flames that lick the depths of our being. But the promise of God is that the force of these uncontrollable circumstances will be replaced by a gentle encounter with the living, gracious, compassionate God. The nature of that encounter is not an impersonal one. We are encountered by a voice—the voice of our Father whose care and concern is for our whole being, mind, body and spirit. As with Elijah, he promises to restore us to wholeness.

The exhaustion and depression that grief causes is by no means the end of our usefulness in the ministry and service of our God. The all-consuming weariness that so often accompanies bereavement is not the end of the journey. Rather, God would have us respond pragmatically. Sleep; eat; drink. Only then will we be in a position to hear the gracious calling of God on our lives. Only then will we be strong enough to work with God in the restoring of our spirituality. There is nothing selfish in pragmatic spirituality. The message of this story about Elijah, in the context of moving through the experience of grief is disarmingly simple: look after Number One.

CHAPTER THREE

THERE IS NOTHING
YOU CAN DO

Psalm 22

O Lord, don't stay away from me! Come quickly to my rescue!
PSALM 22:19

QUO VADIS?

I closed the front door behind me and went quietly back into the living-room. Curling up in the foetal position into my favourite armchair, I stared blankly into space. Eight hours previously, I had commended Clare's body into the hands of God at the crematorium. Friends, family and parishioners had gathered back at the church hall for a buffet meal. The early evening was then spent at home with a closer circle of friends and family. It was getting late and I had just said my farewells to Mum and Dad. Rebekah was in bed, utterly exhausted by the day's events. Now I was on my own.

I had only one thought on my mind. 'What do I do now?' It was a question I was asking about that evening, that week, that month and the rest of my life. For the first time in twenty years, I felt entirely directionless. For the first time in twenty years, I felt utterly and completely alone. While family and friends could support me, there was no one who could carry me into the future. I felt cut off from God. I felt isolated from anyone who might possibly comprehend the agony I was feeling. I felt detached from myself, almost as if I had become an observer somewhere near the ceiling. The only person who could possibly have helped me through this ghastly situation was Clare. But she was dead. I was utterly alone.

THROUGH THE LENS

This is a chapter about one aspect of the impact of Jesus' crucifixion on the grieving process. However, it is a chapter that focuses primarily on Psalm 22. The relationship between Old Testament texts and their apparent fulfilment in the New Testament has been the subject of intense debate throughout the centuries. There is a temptation to interpret the Old Testament in the light of the life and ministry of Jesus. While that may be a valid hermeneutical approach for some texts, it seems to me to be wholly inappropriate as we consider Psalm 22. Rather, it would be better practice to work the other way round—to gain an understanding of the impact that Jesus' death can have on the grieving process in the light of what we learn from this psalm.

The choice to consider Psalm 22 is not an arbitrary one. It is reckoned by biblical scholars that some thirteen allusions are made to the Old Testament in the Gospel passion narratives. Eight of them come from the Psalms and five are from Psalm 22 alone.

My God, my God, why have you abandoned me?
PSALM 22:1

At about three o'clock Jesus cried out with a loud shout, 'Eli, Eli, lema sabachthani?' which means, 'My God, my God, why did you abandon me?'
MATTHEW 27:46

All who see me jeer at me; they stick out their tongues and shake their heads.
PSALM 22:7

People passing by shook their heads and hurled insults at Jesus.
MATTHEW 27:39

'You relied on the Lord,' they say. 'Why doesn't he save you?'
PSALM 22:8

'He trusts in God and claims to be God's Son. Well, then, let us see if God wants to save him now!'
MATTHEW 27:43

My throat is as dry as dust, and my tongue sticks to the roof of my mouth. You have left me for dead in the dust.
PSALM 22:15

Jesus knew that by now everything had been completed; and in order to make the scripture come true, he said, 'I am thirsty.'
JOHN 19:28

They gamble for my clothes and divide them among themselves.
PSALM 22:18

They crucified him and then divided his clothes among them by throwing dice.
MATTHEW 27:35

Psalm 22 was clearly an important passage of scripture for the Gospel writers as they tried to detail the passion of Christ. As we give consideration to it now, we will be in a position to think through one impact of that passion for those who grieve.

It is a moot point as to whether or not Psalm 22 describes a specific incident in the life of a particular individual, probably David. Most scholars would rather view this psalm as a liturgical poem. It was designed for people to use as a reflection on their own circumstances rather than to be considered biographically. If that is the case, it gives an added dimension of power to Jesus' use of the psalm on the cross, for he would then be identifying with sufferers everywhere and throughout all time. Having said that, it is an intensely personal work and undoubtedly reflects individual experience on some level. Calvin, in his *Commentary on the Book of Psalms*, suggested, 'From the tenor of the whole composition, it appears that David does not here refer merely to one persecution, but comprehends all the persecutions which he suffered under Saul.'[6] There are two distinct parts to Psalm 22. The first section, verses 1–21, is primarily an anguished cry for help from a tormented sufferer. The second section, verses 22–31, is a hymn of thanksgiving from the one who has now been rescued from that distress. We must now consider each part in turn.

SEEKING RESTORATION

Underpinning the cry for help that permeates the first 21 verses of this psalm is a complex problem. The writer needed reconciliation and restoration in three areas. First, he needed to be reconciled to himself. There is a very definite sense of the psalmist having lost a sense of direction and physical wholeness. Energy had been sapped and vitality of life had been extinguished: 'My strength is gone, gone like water spilt on the ground. All my bones are out of joint; my heart is like melted wax. My throat is as dry as dust, and my tongue sticks to the roof of my mouth. You have left me for dead in the dust' (vv. 14–15). This description is akin to the agony of Elijah after his confrontation with the prophets of Baal on Mount Carmel. We considered that story in the previous chapter and would not wish to cover the same ground again. Suffice it to say that the psalmist was, quite literally, disintegrated in a physical sense and needed corporeal healing before any spiritual therapy.

Second, the psalmist needed restoration in his relationships with those among whom he lived. He was tormented by the response of others to his condition: 'But I am no longer a human being; I am a worm, despised and scorned by everyone! All who see me jeer at me; they stick out their tongues and shake their heads' (vv. 6–7). Furthermore, he was the victim of violent aggression: 'Many enemies surround me like bulls... They open their mouths like lions, roaring and tearing at me... An evil gang is round me; like a pack of dogs they close in on me; they tear at my hands and feet' (vv. 12–13, 16).

Third, the psalmist needed restoration in his relationship with God. It was this ruptured covenantal bond that lay at the heart of his heartfelt cry in the opening two verses of the psalm: 'My God, my God, why have you abandoned me? I have cried desperately for help, but still it does not come. During the day I call to you, my God, but you do not answer; I call at night, but get no rest.'

The first part of the psalm moves through a number of distinct sections, which perfectly represent the vacillation of emotion that so often characterize the mental state of a believer in crisis. In verses 1–2, the psalmist laments his problem, focusing especially on his sense of God's absenteeism. Next, in verses 3–5, he confesses his trust in God, acknowledging his historic power to save. Thereafter, in verses 6–8, the psalmist laments his problem again and outlines his own feelings of self-hatred. In verses 9–11, he confesses faith in God again, but this time recognizing God's goodness to him personally. Verses 12–18 are a further lamentation, focusing particularly on the ruptured relationships he has with others. Finally, in verses 19–21, he confesses faith once again and acknowledges his utter reliance on God for salvation. There are three issues arising from this section for our purposes.

First, the psalmist may have had an overwhelming sense of being abandoned by God, but that was just not the case. The evidence that interspersed his prayer was that God had never abandoned his people in the past. His personal testimony was of a constant experience of the loving care of God: 'It was you who brought me safely through birth, and when I was a baby, you kept me safe. I have relied on you since the day I was born, and you have always been my God' (vv. 9–10). The importance of this is actually immense. The psalmist may have *felt* abandoned but he *was not* abandoned. Given Jesus' use of the psalm, we are able to infer the same for him—that the Father never did forsake his Son on the cross, even though Jesus *felt* forsaken. What an extraordinary Christian truth we are now able to claim for ourselves! The cry of our Saviour on the cross, 'My God, my God, why have you forsaken me?' is not so much a statement of fact as the outpouring of a very natural human emotion. Christ knew what it was to feel forsaken, so he is able to identify with us in our feelings of forsakenness. But the truth is that God the Father did not actually forsake him, so we can have the absolute confidence that, in our darkest times, he will never forsake us. Viewed in this way, the crucifixion of Christ becomes for us the ultimate example of human anguish being met by the unwavering faithfulness and comfort of God. The cross of Christ becomes for us a sign of hope in grief rather than an ambiguous event suggesting that there may be times when God will abandon us.

Second, the psalmist's personal relationship with God can be understood only within the context of community. In verse 1, the individual nature of that bond is reflected in the way he speaks of 'My God, my God…' Thereafter, he reflects on the manner in which he has continually prayed for deliverance. There is a real sense of private intimacy and reliance upon God expressed here: 'I have cried desperately for help… During the day I call to you, my God… I call at night' (vv. 2–3). Yet, when he tries to comprehend the silent gulf that appears to exist between himself and God, the psalmist draws encouragement primarily from the covenantal relationship between the Creator and his people. He notes that God is 'enthroned as the Holy One, the one whom Israel praises' (v. 3). He reflects on the historic testimony that 'our ancestors put their trust in you; they trusted you, and you saved them' (v. 4).

If the psalmist thought only of his own current experience, there was little reason to continue hoping in God. However, reflection on God's dealings with the faith community as a whole gave him all the evidence he needed to believe that God was still active, still loving and still capable of providing deliverance. That, of course, is the dual-edged sword with which those of us enduring grief have to live. We are regaled with stories from others about how they have been through a similar experience and how God carried them through. There are days when such stories rub salt into our open wound: if God was so good to them, why won't he hear my prayer and give me some peace of mind? There are other days when such stories provide hope for the future: if God was that good to them, maybe he will do the same for me.

Third, there is power in the montage of images that the psalmist uses to express his predicament. I find this a very 'busy' psalm—there is a lot happening, expressed through constantly shifting ideas. This is especially the case from verse 12 through to verse 21. The psalmist describes his enemies as bulls, fierce bulls, wild bulls, lions who roar and tear, a pack of dogs tearing at his hands and feet. He describes himself as a worm, sapped of energy, emaciated, bones out of joint, with a heart like melted wax and a tongue that sticks to the roof of his mouth. The sheer quantity and vivid nature of the images paints for us an abstract picture of the situation in which the psalmist found himself, but does nothing to provide any specific detail. There is a cacophony at work, in the midst of which we find a desperately isolated and hurting human being. That too describes the experience of grief. It is often said that the loneliest place to be is in a crowd. So often those who grieve are in the midst of a whirlpool of activity—preparing for a funeral, clearing out old clothes and possessions, hosting a continual stream of visitors, joining new clubs or associations, sorting out paperwork for the deceased and so on—a cacophony of activity in the midst of which exists an isolated and hurting human being. No amount of hustle and bustle can fill the void left by the death of a loved one. The pain may be dulled for a while but the emptiness remains. The cry of the bereaved to God, in the midst of all the activity, is that of the psalmist in verse 11: 'Do not stay away from me! Trouble is near, and there is no one to help.'

CELEBRATING RESTORATION

While Psalm 22 is best-known for its first verse, it is important to realize that a sense of abandonment from God is not the central message of this portion of scripture. Feeling forsaken is merely the starting point. The latter half of the psalm, verses 22–31, is a wonderful celebration of restoration and a recommitment on behalf of the psalmist to love and serve the Lord as an act of grateful thanksgiving for having heard his cry. This part of the psalm is divided into two clear sections, and we now turn to a brief examination of each one.

The first section, verses 22–26, represents the culmination of the individual/corporate element that we considered above. In contradiction to the first part of the psalm, the writer now rejoices in having been holistically restored. His thankfulness is expressed in a number of different phrases: 'I will tell my people what you have done; I will praise you in their assembly... In the full assembly I will praise you for what you have done... I will offer the sacrifices I promised.' Vitally, the psalmist understood that, having received from God, there was now a responsibility on him to take seriously his role within the community of faith. He had a responsibility to worship and offer sacrifices back to God. But just as importantly, he had a responsibility to tell others what God had done for him. The psalmist was an individual with a story to tell.

All of us who receive healing from God in our grief are individuals with a story to tell that can inspire and encourage others. The great truth that the psalmist grasped is that, despite how he may have felt, he was defined not by God's abandonment of him but by God's presence with him. Earlier, he lamented the fact that others poured scorn on him: 'All who see me jeer at me; they stick out their tongues and shake their head. "You relied on the Lord," they say. "Why doesn't he save you? If the Lord likes you, why doesn't he help you?"' (vv. 7–8). However, that experience of scorn eventually becomes the very foundation of the renewal of his faith: 'He does not neglect the poor or ignore their suffering; he does not turn away from them, but answers when they call for help' (v. 24). I have been asked one particular question more times than I care to remember: 'You have suffered so much through the death of your sister and your wife. How can you possibly still believe in God after all that?' I simply do not understand the question, because what I have experienced of God through my suffering has strengthened my faith in him, not weakened it. Through the bitterness of grief, I have come to understand in new ways the love of God, the grace and mercy of God and the hope that he offers for the future. Like the psalmist, the experience of suffering has become the very foundation for celebration. Like the psalmist, I will not worship God *despite* what I have suffered. Rather, I will worship God *for what he has done for me* through my suffering. I have a story to tell and a sacrifice of praise to offer.

Finally, in verses 27–31, the psalmist recognizes that his experience of restoration is a story that can have an immense impact on the world. As a result of his telling his story to the community of faith, 'All nations will remember the Lord. From every part of the world they will turn to him; all races will worship him' (v. 27). It is not that his story of deliverance will alone bring the nations to faith. It is the fact that the cumulative story of salvation that the faith community owns will have that impact on the world. The psalmist's story is one small part of the wider community story. As we share our stories with each other, so the world will hear of the grace of God and his merciful dealings with us. As we testify to the good things we have experienced, the kingship of God will be proclaimed to all nations and many will be brought to salvation. The restoration that comes to us through the healing of the anguish of grief is a prophetic and eschatological experience. It is prophetic in that it speaks of God's saving activity in the world. It is eschatological in that it is the breaking through of the Kingdom of God into the here and now.

In conclusion, we note that Psalm 22 is primarily a celebration of restoration. First, the psalmist experienced restored relationships with others: previously, he was mocked and jeered but, at the end, he celebrated in the company of the people of God. Second, the psalmist experienced personal restoration: he moved from a deep sense of forsakenness to a profound understanding of his standing before God and the mission and ministry to which he was called. Third, the psalmist experienced restoration with God: whereas he initially lamented the hiddenness of God, at the end he rejoiced in the very presence of his Lord and Saviour. Psalm 22 is one that offers great hope to all those who suffer the anguish of grief. We may feel forsaken now but the hope we have for the future is that our story of the experience of God's grace may be absorbed into the wider community story and may serve as a tool in the kingdom purposes of God. However, there is another, equally profound, way in which this psalm may serve to bring hope to all who grieve. That is found in the manner in which its meaning becomes transformed through the passion of Christ and his death on the cross.

ON MY BEHALF

Matthew 27:46 is one of the most staggering verses in scripture: 'At about three o'clock Jesus cried out with a loud shout, "*Eli, Eli, lema sabachthani*" which means, "My God, my God, why did you abandon me?"' In this one cry is expressed the enormous physical, emotional and spiritual burden that Jesus was carrying on the cross. It was a pitiful cry from a man suffering the most excruciating anguish. As we have already noted, God had not forsaken him, for to do so would negate the hope that we have of a Father who will stand with us in our most testing times. However, Jesus felt forsaken and so he is able to identify with us in our torment.

There are many theories about what Christ actually achieved for us on the cross. It is not my intent to detail those ideas here. What is important for us is the idea that Jesus acted as our substitute; that, in the words of Isaiah 53:4–5, 'he endured the suffering that should have been ours, the pain that we should have borne... We are healed by the punishment he suffered, made whole by the blows he received.' In the context of a theory of substitution, we note that there was a threefold work of restoration for Jesus on the cross. First, Jesus was restored to others. Paul explains this with great clarity in Ephesians 2:11–22, part of which states, 'At that time you were apart from Christ. You were foreigners and did not belong to God's chosen people... But now, in union with Christ Jesus, you who used to be far away have been brought near by the blood of Christ' (vv. 12–13). Second, Jesus was restored to himself on the cross. There can be little doubt that he understood the crucifixion to be the zenith of his ministry; that all else had been leading to this moment. His final words, 'It is finished!' (John 19:30), were not a cry of defeat but an exclamation of victory. In his substitutionary work on the cross, Jesus became whole through the completion of his mission. Third, Jesus was restored to God on the cross. Luke records Jesus' words of restoration and reconciliation: 'Father! In your hands I place my spirit!' (Luke 23:46). After all that he had endured, Jesus was confident of his Father's love and faithfulness. Having felt forsaken a few hours before, Jesus died fully reconciled to God. He had made his own personal journey through the spirituality of Psalm 22.

Since Jesus was acting as our substitute on the cross, the remarkable truth we need to own in our grief is that the work has already been done for us. To be sure, grief leaves us fractured and fragmented. We need to be restored and reconciled to others, ourselves and God. But the liberating reality for those burdened by the exhaustion of grief is that there is nothing we need do in order to achieve that: it has already been done for us. Jesus extends a wonderful invitation to us all: 'Come to me, all of you who are tired from carrying heavy loads, and I will give you rest' (Matthew 11:28). For those who are fatigued through grief, that is good news indeed. We do not need to do anything other than come to Jesus. His restoration is our restoration.

It is the curse of modern expressions of Christianity that, very often, we make humanity the subject of faith. This is expressed through the idea that 'if I believe, a relationship with God can exist'. Making humanity the subject of faith means that reconciliation and restoration ultimately depend on our response to God. However, the view expressed in Psalm 22—and what lies at the heart of the biblical witness—is that God is the subject of faith. Restoration and reconciliation are not dependent on our response at all. Rather, they are dependent solely on the gracious activity of God in our lives. This understanding is vital for those who are tired out by the excessive emotional demands of grief. The thought of having to 'do something' in order to be restored is a terrible concept when we are too tired even to open our eyes in the morning or hold a conversation with friends and family. The good news is that there is nothing we need to do. God is the subject and he has done everything that needs doing through the substitutionary death of Christ. If we despair of God in the depths of grief, we cannot break free from him. If we feel utterly forsaken and rail against him for his apparent absenteeism, God will not let us go. He loves us too much for that.

If we are able to cling to God even when it seems like there is no God, like the psalmist we will know victory. The testimony of Psalm 22—the testimony of Jesus on the cross—is that victory is integrally intertwined with the refusal to believe that God has forsaken us, even when we may feel forsaken. When grief overwhelms us, we need to cling to the great promise recorded in Romans 8:35–39:

Who, then, can separate us from the love of Christ? Can trouble do it, or hardship or persecution or hunger or poverty or danger or death?... No, in all these things we have complete victory through him who loved us! For I am certain that nothing can separate us from his love: neither death nor life, neither angels nor other heavenly rulers or powers, neither the present nor the future, neither the world above nor the world below—there is nothing in all creation that will ever be able to separate us from the love of God which is ours through Christ Jesus our Lord.

There is nothing you can do to achieve restoration and reconciliation with others, yourself and God. Jesus has done it all for you. Rest in that.

CHAPTER FOUR

AN EMBARRASSING SILENCE
AND A SHUFFLE OF FEET

John 11:38-44

Jesus said to Martha, 'Didn't I tell you that you would see God's glory if you believed?'
JOHN 11:40

There was one ambition that Clare held dear to her heart more than any other—to make a personal and private pilgrimage to Israel. She did not want to go as part of a package tour, nor even with a local church. Her desire was for just the two of us to walk in Jesus' footsteps together. Two things, however, were preventing us from doing that. First, would it be practical to go on our own? To be sure, we had spent three months travelling in India together but that was before her illness. Things were very different now, with tablets to take and periodic epileptic fits to endure. Second, our journeying abroad had been abandoned because it had become nigh on impossible to arrange suitable travel insurance. As Clare's condition continued, the idea of Israel began to fade from her mind. It was an unobtainable pipe dream rather than a vision to be realized.

However, a strange series of events led us to meet with a Palestinian bishop who kindly offered to host us with a monastic order in Jerusalem for the duration of a visit. Furthermore, he offered to take personal financial responsibility should Clare become ill, so insurance was not required. With grateful hearts and tremendous excitement, we boarded the plane bound for Tel Aviv airport in January 1998.

Our brief time of pilgrimage was a tremendous experience. Jerusalem, Bethlehem, Galilee, Capernaum, Jericho and Nazareth were among the places we visited. Each one had a profound impact upon us. God had much to say and there was so much we needed to hear from him. Ironically, though, the most insightful moment between God and me was in the little town of Bethany, a few short miles south-east of Jerusalem. It was here that I was to be brought to a most interesting realization about the story of the raising of Lazarus—a realization that strongly influenced how I dealt with Clare's condition and my subsequent grief after her death.

AN UNEXPECTED SCRIPTURAL ENCOUNTER

God has a great sense of humour. So often, he speaks to us in the way we least expect, even in the way we least want. Frankly, the story of the raising of Lazarus from John 11 was one that had grated with me throughout Clare's illness. These miracles were fine to read about—but where was the power of Jesus now, when we needed it the most? I always felt like I was missing out on the miraculous. Christian members of our family, and close friends, regaled us on a regular basis about the people they had seen healed at their churches. They would excitedly phone with stories they had heard from a friend of a friend of a friend who, in their church, had seen someone with a brain tumour healed. Clare smiled kindly and listened politely. Later, she would be quiet or I would find her lying on our bed, gently sobbing. These people meant well; they were trying to offer some hope; but all they succeeded in doing was to compound Clare's sense of failure at not being healed.

We soon began to realize that sometimes, the people who talked to us about these things, and more often those who came to pray with us, were actually running to their own agenda, not ours. On one occasion, a Christian that I vaguely knew from another church came to visit. He had only recently discovered the nature of Clare's condition. We were touched that he had put himself out to come round and see us. He sat down on the sofa and came straight to the point. 'Now, about this tumour. Have you thought about praying for God's healing?'

Clare and I looked at each other, flabbergasted, and tried hard to suppress our laughter. Tempted to say, 'Do you know, we hadn't thought about trying that!' instead I said, 'Well, we have been praying for some years now but continue to trust God in this.'

He leant forward earnestly. 'No, have you *really* prayed? Have you *claimed* God's healing? Have you spoken out with authority, claiming Jesus' victory over death?'

It became clear to me. Our Christian brother was not asking if we had prayed: he was asking if we had prayed *his way*. Seemingly, we had been using the wrong 'method' and we needed him to 'do it right' for us. Then Clare would be healed. I wanted to challenge him about this but Clare, sensing what I was about to say, got in first. She thanked him for his interest and concern and asked him to pray for her.

His prayer lasted a long, long time. He prayed quietly. He prayed loudly. He spoke with authority, demanding that Jesus Christ claim the victory in this situation. His prayer became an exposition of the story of the raising of Lazarus. As Jesus had overcome the forces of death for that man, so he would do the same for Clare, if only she would believe. When he had finished, he exhorted Clare to 'claim the victory' and then left. We never saw him again.

One unfortunate aspect of that encounter was that I developed an aversion to the story of the raising of Lazarus, but that would change as I stood in Bethany on a crisp morning in January 1998.

A DIFFICULT STORY

The story of the raising of Lazarus is the greatest of Jesus' 'signs', designed to reveal his glory, as recorded in John's Gospel. It is to be understood as a prophetic act, signalling the power of God over death, and as a precursor to the resurrection of Jesus Christ himself.

Notwithstanding the obvious link with his resurrection, the story itself is an intriguing episode in the life and ministry of Jesus.

Jesus had left Jerusalem and was preparing to return for his final Passover. While he was preparing, word came from Mary and Martha that their brother Lazarus was ill. The message they sent was brief—'Lord, your dear friend is ill' (v. 3)—and there is no hint that they wanted Jesus to visit. Perhaps they understood the danger he would have been in by returning to the vicinity of Jerusalem. Nevertheless, there was clearly an expectation that Jesus would do something for Lazarus—heal him with a distant word, perhaps. Jesus' response is unexpected. First, he tarries: 'Yet when he received the news that Lazarus was ill, he stayed where he was for two more days' (v. 6). Given the implicit urgency of the message, and the extra detail that the messenger would no doubt have provided concerning Lazarus' condition, it seems bizarre that Jesus would not respond immediately. Second, Jesus turns Lazarus' condition into an opportunity for theological learning. 'The final result of this illness will not be the death of Lazarus; this has happened in order to bring glory to God, and it will be the means by which the Son of God will receive glory' (v. 4).

Now here is a further point at which I struggled with this story. In my head, I could understand the inactivity of Jesus and his desire to bring glory to God by waiting until Lazarus had died and then performing the ultimate miracle. But in my heart, I could not understand why a man of compassion should allow the family of Lazarus to go through so much pain before responding to their need. On reflection, I understand that this was not really a criticism of Jesus so much as a sense of frustration with my own utter helplessness while watching someone I loved suffer so much. Ironically, the sufferer is often able to live quite peaceably with the condition and find God within that. Many sufferers can empathize with Joni Eareckson Tada's sentiments in *A Step Further* that, 'I do not care if I am confined to this wheelchair provided from it I can bring glory to God.'[7] More often than not, it is the carer rather than the victim who struggles to reach that point of spiritual equanimity.

Our frustration at being so utterly helpless turns into a railing against Jesus for not doing enough to respond to the situation. Certainly, I felt helpless watching Clare deteriorate as the years went by and, in my heart, transposed that helplessness into anger at Jesus' inactivity. This story about Lazarus did nothing to assuage my feelings. Yet running parallel with those negative feelings was an absolute trust in the sovereignty of God and his power to bring victory out of defeat. I was caught in the same paradox of faith as Martha: 'If you had been here, Lord, my brother would not have died! But I know that even now God will give you whatever you ask him for' (vv. 21–22).

THE WAITING GAME

The atmosphere surrounding Jesus' miracle at Bethany was clearly one of suspicion and distrust. Martha had voiced her disappointment. Mary, in verse 32, expressed the same sentiment: 'Lord, if you had been here, my brother would not have died!' The mourners, too, were disenchanted with Jesus: 'He gave sight to the blind man, didn't he? Could he not have kept Lazarus from dying?' (v. 37). Not surprising, then, that when Jesus ordered the stone to be rolled away from the entrance to the cave, Martha was completely indignant: 'There will be a bad smell, Lord. He has been buried four days!' (v. 39). In her heart, Martha probably thought that Jesus had done enough damage by not coming sooner to heal. Now he wanted to embarrass the family further by messing with the corpse. But Jesus rebuked her: 'Didn't I tell you that you would see God's glory if you believed?' (v. 40). Martha, caught in this paradox between faith and unbelief, ordered the stone to be rolled away. Jesus prayed to his Father in heaven and then called out in a loud voice, 'Lazarus, come out!'

When I visited Bethany, I had the privilege of going into Lazarus' tomb. The entrance is small; I needed to crouch slightly to go through the 'door'. Upon entering, there were about twenty steps circling down a level. Gingerly making my way down these rough steps hewn from the rock, I entered a small ante-chamber, presumably where the body would have been prepared. Thereafter, I had to go on hands and knees to crawl under a ledge to enter the burial chamber itself—a small room with a 'bed' of rock upon which the body of Lazarus would have lain.

I sat on the 'bed' and prayed. I imagined myself into the story. I imagined the scene outside, as Jesus stood near the entrance with excited but nervous disciples, a disbelieving crowd of mourners and a family torn apart by a confusing emotional mix of un-contained grief and irrepressible hope. I imagined the authoritative cry of Jesus, 'Lazarus, come out!'

Then it struck me. At the word of Jesus—certainly not before—the corpse would have awoken. Lazarus would have slowly become conscious of his surroundings. What emotions would have filled his clouded brain? Fear, confusion, amazement, exhilaration and so much more. Slowly, he would have risen to his feet, body stiff from four days of lying inactive, pins and needles coursing through his limbs as blood started to circulate once more. Lazarus would have struggled on to all fours to crawl under the ledge and stumble through the ante-chamber. Carefully, he would have made his way up the steps. We read in verse 44 that his hands and feet were still wrapped and that he had a cloth covering his face. Lazarus would have had to make his way up the uneven steps very slowly in order to avoid tumbling. Only then could he appear at the mouth of the cave.

What of the scene outside the burial cave? Jesus stood in the midst of this highly charged atmosphere and cried, 'Lazarus, come out!' Silence. They waited. They waited. Unaware of the activity within the burial chamber, the embarrassing silence would have been deafening. The disciples would have shuffled their feet, nerv-ously thinking that maybe this time Jesus had bitten off more than he could chew. They waited. Mary and Martha would have looked askance at Jesus, wondering why he was putting them through all this agony. They waited. Silence. The crowd of mourners would have been seething that Jesus should have the audacity to mess with Mary and Martha's emotions in such a public and humiliating way. They waited. The silence grew louder.

And then Lazarus came out. The scene changed completely.

But the spiritual lesson for me in Bethany was in comprehending the waiting. I had always imagined Jesus to call Lazarus out and— hey presto!—there he was! In reality, Jesus called and then they would have had to wait maybe five minutes or more to see the miracle. Only five minutes; but five minutes that would have seemed a lifetime. Most importantly, how they reacted in that five minutes of waiting would determine the depth and degree of faith they had in Jesus.

FIVE MINUTES OF FAITH

Reflecting on this passage in the wake of Clare's death, I thought that my five minutes had lasted eight years. From the moment of her diagnosis to the moment she died beside me, I was standing with Jesus at the entrance to the darkened cave, waiting on him to perform a miracle. I now realize, however, that my five minutes only began at the moment of Clare's death and that they are an ongoing experience in the midst of my grief.

The bitterness of grief is a time of waiting on God. There is so much silence in grief. There is so much waiting. There seems to be so much inactivity by God. As the disciples stood outside the tomb in an embarrassing silence and shuffling their feet nervously, so the experience of grief is often just a time to stand with Jesus, waiting for something positive to happen. Anything will do, Lord. Just do something in my life to show me that you are in control! We cannot see what resurrection activity is occurring inside the tomb of our hearts; often we have no sense of the new life stirring within us. We merely stand and wait. We watch Jesus and we shuffle our feet.

The ultimate test of grief is how we respond to Jesus during the five minutes of waiting. There are times when each of the players in this story is reflected in our behaviour and thoughts. We experience the paradoxical mixture of pain and ultimate trust of Mary and Martha. We feel the seething anger of the crowd of mourners as they stare incredulously at Jesus' bizarre behaviour. We admit, with the disciples, to doubting the power of Jesus, as the minutes tick by and the silence increases and the waiting grows longer. In grief, the seconds seem like minutes, the minutes seem like hours, the hours seem like days, the days seem like months and the months seem like years. Time drags by and we long for the emptiness in our hearts to be filled with a miracle from God—the tangible presence of Jesus. We know he is with us but we struggle to feel him with us. Grief is an experience of a void of feeling—standing at the tomb, waiting for new life to burst forth, but just feeling barren and empty inside.

Sarah Doudney, in *Psalms of Life*, had it right:

> *But the waiting time, my brothers,*
> *Is the hardest time of all.*[8]

A CONTROLLED GRIEF

It has become important for me to learn that waiting on God is not the same thing as experiencing the inactivity of God. Even in the silent times, the Spirit of God is extremely active, rebuilding my world and bringing healing. While the crowds and the relatives and the disciples stood impassively outside the cave, Lazarus was extremely busy inside! The silence of their perspective did not contain the whole truth of what was happening in Bethany at that moment. They were unable to see inside the tomb and so could not see the ongoing resurrection activity. So it is with us, that comprehending the healing and renewing work of God is most often retrospective: we look back and we see how far God has brought us rather than being able to discern movement at any given moment in time.

For this reason, it is absolutely vital to go through the grieving process at a pace appropriate to the griever rather than at the suggested or enforced pace of others. It is essential to retain control over your own grief. I will never forget the words of one member of my congregation, only three weeks after the funeral service of my sister: 'Have you got over Jackie yet?' Such gross insensitivity was actually born out of a misunderstanding of the silence of grief. Because my grieving was not visible, he assumed that my grieving was finished. He was standing outside Lazarus' tomb. The activity of God was going on inside.

Ultimately, of course, we move through the grieving process in God's timing. I am constantly amazed at the continually shifting patterns of grief. How I felt eight months after Clare's death was so very different from how I felt three months previously. Issues I could not have faced in the immediate aftermath, I could face a few months later. The prophecy in Isaiah applied to Jesus' healing ministry in Matthew 12:20 is most profound: 'A bruised reed he will not break, and a smouldering wick he will not snuff out.' The word for bruised, *suntribo*, does not describe the result of a punch so much as the result of a consistent rubbing and grinding. The experience of grief is just that. Grief is not a single body-blow that bruises. It is a mental, spiritual and emotional bruising through a grinding and rubbing process. It is continual. It is sore. God takes into account the fact that those rubbed raw in grief are on the verge of breaking. So the healing process cannot be rushed: it is slow, it is deliberate, it is gradual—at times the movement is almost indiscernible—but always the Spirit of God is working for renewal and resurrection.

Perhaps the most misunderstood hallmark of grief is the wait-ing in silence. Those standing outside the tomb have no way of comprehending what is going on inside. For Mary and Martha, the waiting lasted only five minutes. For others, those five minutes will continue for many years. How we respond to Jesus in those five minutes of waiting is the true test of faith. We must learn not to judge the activity of God by what we can see. Instead, we must learn to perceive the activity of God through the eyes of faith and trust his timing in the process of resurrection. The challenge of Jesus to Martha is made to everyone who grieves: 'Didn't I tell you that you would see God's glory if you believed?' (v. 40). The waiting time is indeed the hardest time of all, but waiting in patience and faith will bear witness to personal resurrection and the glory of God.

CHAPTER FIVE

THE FIGHT OF YOUR LIFE!

Genesis 32:22-32

'Your name will no longer be Jacob. You have struggled with God and with men, and you have won; so your name will be Israel.'
GENESIS 32:28

LEARNING A LESSON WITH FORREST GUMP

A year after Clare's death, Rebekah and I went on holiday to California. We stayed with a good friend who made sure that we traversed the Californian highways in real style and saw just about all we could fit into a fortnight's stay. Part of the time was spent in Monterey, a beautiful seaside town. Our friend Roy had to go to work that morning, so Rebekah and I went out on a three-hour whale-watching trip, visited the local aquarium and meandered through the delightful shopping areas. Before long, we came across the Bubba Gump Shrimping Company. I looked quizzically at the logo, feeling sure I had seen it somewhere before. Then it dawned on me. The Bubba Gump Shrimping Company was a fictional place from the movie *Forrest Gump*. Bubba and Gump were military comrades during the Vietnam War and had decided to set up a shrimping business when they were sent home. Bubba died in combat but Gump set up the company in honour of his fallen brother, giving half the proceeds to the dead man's family. To my astonishment, as I looked at the factory, there was Forrest Gump! He was sitting on a bench in that familiar white suit, clutching a box of chocolates. For no price at all, you could sit with him and have your photograph taken. Rebekah, who had seen the film, was thrilled at this opportunity, so we made our way over and joined the queue. After five minutes of waiting, it was our turn. Rebekah sat next to Forrest and I sat alongside her.

'My name is Forrest—Forrest Gump,' the character intoned in that instantly recognizable drawl.

'Hello, I'm Rebekah. I've come from England.'

'Well, ain't that nice? Would you like a chocolate? Momma always said, "Life's like a box of chocolates. You never know what you're gonna get!"'

Rebekah took a chocolate and popped it into her mouth. Forrest turned to her and smiled.

'Well, Rebekah, who gives your dad more trouble—you or your mum?'

My heart sank, awaiting the inevitable response. Rebekah glanced briefly up at me and then turned to Forrest Gump.

'Er… I do, I think!'

'Well, does your momma not give your dad any trouble too?'

'No, not really. She's very good.'

'I bet your parents are real proud of you. Is Momma here with you today?'

Rebekah paused. 'No, she's not with us right now.'

'OK. Well, you have a real good holiday, y'hear? Say hi to England for me when you get back.'

'Thanks, Forrest. I will. And thank you for the chocolate.'

We walked off, holding hands but not saying too much. I wasn't sure where to take the conversation after that.

We chatted for a bit about various things and then I turned to Rebekah.

'Sweetheart, you didn't tell him that Mummy was dead, did you?'

'No, there was no point.'

'Why not?'

'Well, I'm never going to see him again and there's no point upsetting him, is there?'

WHO AM I?

I met Clare when I was seventeen. I was 34 when she died. In the period that we were together, we created a great deal of shared history—some of it bad, but for the most part good and enjoyable. We went through A' Levels together. She supported me as I studied for a first degree and, subsequently, a Master's and PhD. We lived variously in Guildford, Nottingham, Birmingham and London. We had seven different jobs between us during that time. We visited overseas. We knew the pain of near bankruptcy and the joy of parenthood. To all intents and purposes, we were not Steve and Clare. We were 'SteveandClare'—bonded together under God in a most special way. When Clare died, half of me died with her. I do not mean that in any romantic sense. I believe it to be theologically true. It was not until after her death that I finally understood Genesis 2:24: 'A man leaves his father and mother and is united with his wife, and they become one.' There is a definite unity that becomes real in a lifelong partnership commitment.

The rupturing of this unity—and the loss of part of myself—became apparent in a number of different ways. The most notice-able problem came while reminiscing with Rebekah or with friends about our time together. At first, I thought I was losing my mind: I didn't seem to remember anything very well. Rebekah would ask about her early years and I would only have hazy recollections. I would sit with close friends and we would chat about events from years gone by but I would not have much clarity of detail. Finally, it dawned on me that I was not losing my mind. Rather, half my memory had been wiped out. When Clare was alive, we would bounce memories off each other in conversation.

'Do you remember going out for that meal with Johnny and Helen in Chichester?'

'Oh yes, it was a Chinese, wasn't it?'

'No, it was an Indian.'

'Oh, that's right. That's where the waiter brought the beer over with a lump of glass in it.'

'That's right! I'd forgotten about that!'

And so conversations would continue—the shared memory bank exchanging details in order to present a complete picture. With Clare gone, however, I was left with only half the memories.

I also noticed with surprise and dismay that some friends treated me as 'incomplete'. A definite awkwardness existed where previously there had been a relaxed air. Dinner invitations decreased. The phone stopped ringing. I soon came to realize who my most trusted and loyal friends were—and, in some cases, I was surprised by the discovery. To be sure, I could have put more energy into keeping in touch, but the depression caused by grief leads to a social disabling beyond anything I could previously have imagined. I was too tired to talk. I could not face making the first move to initiate conversations and friendships. Even now, some considerable time after Clare's death, I still find it difficult to be proactive in social interaction.

Most profoundly, though, I did not know who I was any more. I had been 'SteveandClare'. I had been one half of a partnership since my teens. To all intents and purposes, I had never been single. I had no other point of reference. My identity was 'SteveandClare' and, without my wife, I did not know what it meant to be 'Steve'. The struggle to find a new identity was subconscious but intensive. I could not define myself outside of that relationship and so began to define myself as a grieving widower. Rather comically, I sought every opportunity to reinforce that definition. I would talk about Clare dying in every conversation. I would meet new people and find myself manufacturing the flow of conversation so as to be able to say, 'My wife has just died.' I would tell taxi drivers about my loss. I would phone companies rather than write to inform them of Clare's death, just so that I could say the words. I would use marital anecdotes in my lecturing at college. In retrospect, I do not think I was looking for sympathy. I just did not know who I was any more. I was drowning in a sea of ambiguity and was desperately reaching out for some personal clarity.

I recognized what I was doing at quite an early stage. I also recognized that it was an important part of the grief process and was not to be denied. I therefore set myself a time limit on such behaviour. Clare died in July. I decided that it would be personally acceptable to indulge in such behaviour until 30 November. Thereafter, I would make a conscious effort not to define myself in those terms. If the death of my wife came up in conversation, fine, but I would no longer drive conversations to that conclusion. I would not tell strangers about what had happened unless absolutely necessary. If asked about my marital status, I would say that I was single. This was not to deny my past; it was a question of forming a healthy identity that could undergird my healing.

The attempt to find personal definition in the face of such loss is perfectly natural. It is a vital aspect of the grieving process. In my ministerial capacity, I am in constant contact with individuals who are doing just this. Sadly, however, many never work through this phase. It is vital to learn to redefine ourselves after such a traumatic loss. That is why I began this chapter with the story of Rebekah and Forrest Gump. Like me, Rebekah had spent the first year telling everyone who would listen that Clare had died. Not only were such conversations cathartic, Rebekah soon learnt, as any eight-year-old would, that sympathy could be elicited that way—which inevitably resulted in hugs and kisses, sweets and cuddly toys. I took it as a sign of tremendous personal maturity when she consciously chose not to tell Forrest Gump of her loss. She did not seek to define herself as a grieving daughter. She did not seek sympathy from this character. She did not try to get an extra chocolate from him in this way. Rather, she considered the impact that such disclosure would have on him, set that response within the context of their transient relationship and decided to give an ambiguous reply. I was proud of Rebekah that day. Through that encounter with Forrest Gump, Rebekah grew up in grief.

REFINED, NOT DEFINED

The story of Jacob wrestling, recorded in Genesis 32:22–32, is one of the most variously interpreted stories in the Bible. The ambiguous fashion in which the story is written allows for much imaginative play in seeking its meaning. Whatever the author's original intent, it does have much to say about the formation of personal identity under the refining hand of God.

Integral to the power of this story is the fact that the identity of Jacob's adversary is never made explicit. Presumably he is God or a messenger of God but verse 24 merely notes that '...a man came and wrestled with him until just before daybreak'. In verse 29, Jacob asks the name of his combatant but the request for information is neatly sidestepped. Given that the wrestling took place at night, there is a shadowy air to the story. The man's name is not known; his face is not seen. The reason for the wrestling is never made clear. Details of the fight are not given. Several hours of turmoil are neatly summarized in just one brief sentence. In narrative terms, the struggle itself is not important, but the outcome of this extraordinary event most certainly is. There are six pertinent issues to draw from this passage with regard to the grieving process.

First, the shadowy hiddenness of the adversary is no mere detail. Rather, it is a very important factor for us as we consider grief in the context of this passage. The truth about the grieving process is that the wrestling involved is so often against obscured or concealed emotional enemies. Because Clare had been ill for eight years, I was reasonably well prepared for her death. However, I was—and continue to be—caught off-guard on a regular basis by various assaults on the mind and emotions. I can be depressed and not know why. I can cry for no reason. Completely contrary to my previous behaviour, I have become very weepy at films: much to my daughter's embarrassment, I have even been known to blub at the latest Disney epic at the cinema. I can get angry over trivial things; I can get angry at nothing. On occasions, my temper is completely disproportionate to the provocation. Often, I cannot be bothered seeing friends or making contact with them and I do not know why. My most troubling experiences within the grieving process have been to do with the concealed and the unknown: 'Why do I feel like this today? There just seems to be no reason for it.'

Second, the dialogue between Jacob and the man is quite significant. Three times they interact in conversation and each time there is a different balance of power. Verse 26 is the first example to consider.

'The man said, "Let me go; daylight is coming."

"I won't, unless you bless me," Jacob answered.'

The extraordinary truth here is that Jacob was proving the stronger combatant! After hours of struggle with this divine visitor, Jacob had the physical advantage. The man asked to be released but, with extraordinary boldness, Jacob attached a condition to that release. He was not denied but he would have to wait for a while longer.

In the second exchange, verses 27–28, it is the divine visitor who appears stronger:

'"What is your name?" the man asked.

"Jacob," he answered.

The man said, "Your name will no longer be Jacob. You have struggled with God and with men, and you have won; so your name will be Israel."'

We will consider the details of this exchange below. It is enough at this point to note that the stranger now has the advantage and dictates the flow of the conversation. Finally, in verse 29, it is Jacob who takes the initiative by asking for the man's name. This is denied him but he does receive the blessing for which he had yearned.

What is so pertinent for us is the very fact that, in the midst of the struggle, there was a dialogue between Jacob and God. The tussle was not carried out in silence. Furthermore, there was a deferential intimacy between the two combatants. Each requested personal information and activity from the other without losing a sense of respect. In the midst of the struggle to come to terms with grief, we are able to talk openly with God. He neither silently nor passively observes us in our time of trial. We are able to talk with him about the deep things and to request his blessing.

Third, and related to what we have just noted, there was a real evenness between Jacob and God in this struggle. It is a quite extraordinary situation where a man can equal God in combat. It is an even more extraordinary truth that we worship a God who will allow himself to become weak in order to strengthen and bless us! When we struggle in grief, God does not relate to us with an attitude of superiority. To be sure, he remains sovereign, but he does not cling to dominance. Rather, God is prepared to sweat and toil and fight with and alongside us. He questions and encourages us to question him. Something quite extraordinary is related in this story. Jacob wrestles with God, prevails against him, and receives a blessing and a new name. God is cast in the role of giver. There is no neat boundary drawn in this interaction. Jacob is strong and God is weak. Yet in another sense, God prevails too and, from his position of strength, bestows a blessing on Jacob. It is a disquieting story in that it refuses to endorse our understanding of God as strong, superior, untouchable and inviolable. But the sovereign vulnerability of God also liberates us to be honest with him and entrust ourselves to him. His strength is in his weakness. His sovereignty is underpinned by the fact that he understands the struggle and has engaged with it himself.

Fourth, Jacob received a new name as a result of this wrestling match. Names were very important in biblical times, since they reflected the nature of the person. That being the case, the giving of a new name indicated that, through the struggle, Jacob had become a new person. He had asked for a blessing but received so much more. The name Jacob derives from the Hebrew for 'cheat' or 'trickster'. Given the events of Genesis 27, in which Jacob stole a blessing from Isaac, it was an appropriate name. Now, Jacob had wrestled with God and had implored him for a blessing. The name Israel is slightly ambiguous. However, it is rooted in the idea that 'God preserves' or 'God protects'. The cheater had become the protected child. Through the struggle, his character had changed and his relationship with God had changed. Jacob/Israel had forged a new identity in the pain.

Fifth, it is interesting that Jacob had the new name imposed on him. He did not ask for it. The imposition was the result of a decision made solely by the sovereign God. Indeed, Jacob had not asked for this encounter at all; it just happened to him. Yet, as an act of grace, God had redeemed Jacob through the struggle and made him a new person. The experience of bereavement is an imposition on us. We do not seek it; we do not enjoy it. Yet God is able to redeem us and renew us through the struggle, and we sit under his sovereignty in doing that.

Sixth, and perhaps most importantly, the person of Jacob/Israel became defined by *the name that resulted from the struggle*. He was not defined by *the struggle itself*. There is a subtle nuance here but it is a vital one all the same. As we noted at the beginning of this chapter, there is a temptation for us to seek personal identity and definition in the struggle of grief. I may want to define myself as a widower. Rebekah may wish to define herself as a grieving daughter. The struggle of grief may become the moment or event of self-definition. It may become the focal point of self-identity. However, Jacob shows us a better way under the gracious activity of God. Jacob did not become defined by the struggle. Rather, he became defined by the name that he received as a result of the struggle: 'You have struggled with God and with men, and you have won; so your name will be Israel' (v. 28). If the etymology of 'Israel' relates to the protection and loving care of God, it is that which marked the identity of the growth of the nation throughout subsequent biblical history. This is vital for us to grasp as we struggle through the grieving process, because it shifts the formation of identity from a human experience to a divine encounter. If we allow our identity and our self-understanding to be defined by the event, we will never escape from the trauma of it. Healing will prove impossible. If, however, we allow our identity and self-understanding to be defined by our relationship with the God who seeks to protect us and offer grace and mercy to us, we will be able to move forward and receive healing.

Refusing to be defined by the event itself is not to deny its impact upon us. There are those close to me who have difficulty understanding my passionate intention not to allow the death of Clare to define who I am and how I think of myself. Some clearly believe that I am in denial. Others cannot understand how I have 'got over it so quickly'. The truth is this: I shall never get over losing Clare. However, I do not believe it to be God's will for me to seek personal reference through the trauma of loss instead of his sovereign and healing grace. The struggle of grief has served to refine me but I will not allow it to define me. The example of Jacob is of a man who was refined by the wrestling but defined by the name. He never 'got over' the wrestling. In verse 31 we read, 'The sun rose as Jacob was leaving Peniel, and he was limping because of his hip.' After this divine encounter, Jacob was not the same as he was before and he had the limp to prove it. Those of us who suffer the trauma of grief will limp for the rest of our lives, but we have a choice. We can either seek our identity in being a cripple or we can view the limp as a reminder of God's gracious activity in our lives. Be defined or be refined: the choice is ours.

A DIVINE CRIPPLING

There is a harsh truth for us that underscores this story in Genesis 32. The truth is that the new name, the new identity, is integrally intertwined with the crippling encounter. Jacob could not have been refined or matured without the pain. As Brueggemann wrote in his book, *Genesis*, 'Jacob is a cripple with a blessing.'[9] Victory and defeat were inextricably entwined as a result of this encounter. Jacob was defeated in that he had to limp for the rest of his life, yet he was victorious in that he had received the blessing he longed for and so much more besides.

This, of course, is the way of God. This is the example of Christ to us. The God who forsook his glory to be born in a stable; the God who lived among us and was forsaken, misunderstood, mistreated; the God who hung on the cross and died a criminal's death; the God who was buried in a common grave: this is the God who constantly embraces defeat in order to pave the way for victory. The example of Christ to us is none other than an example of finding victory in defeat. Jesus is the ultimate cripple with a blessing. It is through his crippling that we can be healed.

None of us would choose the pain of bereavement. None of us would wish to go through the agony and trauma of watching a loved one die. There is no experience comparable to the pain of holding a spouse or child or parent or friend in your arms as they die. There are no words to describe the anguish that seems to fill the years and months and weeks and days and hours and minutes and seconds that follow on from that event. However, we do have a choice as to how that pain may be utilized. We can choose to let it be either refining or defining. It may seem a subtle distinction when we are in the thick of the fight but it is a vital distinction all the same. Ultimately, our ability to make this distinction will either prevent the healing process or allow it to begin.

Verse 30 is so beautiful. 'Jacob said, "I have seen God face to face, and I am still alive"; so he named the place Peniel.' He had struggled for hours. He had been wounded and was walking with a painful limp. Yet his response was to find God in the midst of the pain and rejoice in the encounter. There was no hint of bitterness or anger at the events that he had endured so courageously. He was a man at peace with himself and at peace with his God. It is no coincidence that this story immediately precedes the narrative about his reconciliation with Esau. The peace of God that passes all understanding infuses our soul and flows out in forgiveness and reconciliation with others. There is often so much hurt and anger and bitterness within families who are trying to cope with a bereavement situation. This portion of scripture clearly shows the way forward. A physically crippled Jacob stands face to face with his emotionally crippled brother in the presence of a God who is willing to be crippled for them both—for us all. When we are prepared to embrace our crippled natures as an aspect of the divine, it is then that families and individuals can be healed.

There is victory in defeat. There is no other way. We must choose to be refined or defined. We must choose wisely.

CHAPTER SIX

LOOK BACK IN ANGER

Psalm 137

Happy are those who pay you back for what you have done to us—who take your babies and smash them against a rock.
PSALM 137:8b–9

BETTER TRAINING REQUIRED?

Clare and I were peaceful for the first time in a month. We had received the diagnosis four weeks previously and the news had not been good. No surgery was possible. Radiotherapy and chemo-therapy would have no real impact on a tumour that size and of that nature. The best that could be offered was palliative care until the inevitable happened—two months at worst, about six months at best. We had begun making the preparations and were trying to adjust to this tumultuous news when, late one morning, the phone rang. It was the neurological unit at the hospital. The neurosurgeon had taken a further look at the X-rays and had now decided that surgery would be possible after all. We needed to come and see him as soon as possible to talk the matter over and make the arrangements.

We drove the twenty miles or so in the confident knowledge that, although things would never be the same again, at least we would have more time together. At least Clare would see Rebekah grow up. We went into the hospital and sat with the other patients in the waiting area. Three times the neurosurgeon came out and hurried past us. An hour came and went. The hustle and bustle of the neurological unit went on around us and we became increasingly nervous and uneasy. Eventually, a nurse came out of the surgery and beckoned us in.

As we entered the room, the nurse sat down quietly on a chair behind us. We sat before a desk and waited. The nurse said nothing and we were surprised a few moments later when a doctor not known to us entered, rather than the neurosurgeon himself. Clare and I clasped hands together as he sat down on the other side of the desk. He did not make any eye contact but launched into a highly technical description of Clare's condition that left us completely baffled. Eventually, he paused and briefly looked towards Clare.

'I'm sorry, but all this means we won't be able to operate after all. There really is nothing that can be done for you.'

We were stunned. For nearly a month we had been trying to get used to the inevitability of Clare's impending death. We had sorted out our differences; we had dealt with any skeletons left in the cupboard. More pragmatically, we had sorted out our finances and planned the funeral service. The news that surgery would be happening had then transformed our world—there was hope again. Now, here was some anonymous doctor, without the ability to explain clearly and with no desire to make eye contact, telling us it had all been a ghastly mistake. As if that was not bad enough, his concluding comments left us absolutely flabbergasted. Clare looked at him with tears in her eyes and said, 'I'm going to die, aren't I?'

He picked up a pen and started writing on a pad of paper before saying in a most offhand way, 'We're all dying, pet.'

He could not have been more offensive or hurtful if he had tried. I wanted to punch him. I wanted to pin him up against the wall and grab him by the throat until he apologized to my wife. I wanted to hurt him as much as his brusque comment had hurt Clare. But we stood up, shook him by the hand, thanked him for his time and left the surgery.

We drove home in silence, scarcely able to take in the events of that ten-minute consultation.

THE HIDDEN ENEMY

I was with a close friend a week ago, telling her how the writing of this book was progressing. I mentioned that I would soon be starting a chapter on anger and that I would find it an especially hard one to write.

'Why's that?' she asked.

'Well, it's not something I've ever really had a problem with. I've never been that angry about Clare's death.'

My friend, who knows me so well, was quiet for a few moments. 'Oh,' she said casually, 'you weren't even angry when Clare was first diagnosed?'

'No,' I replied. 'Not even then.'

In her consummate wisdom, my friend decided to say nothing. We were silent for a few moments and the conversation moved on.

But I was troubled for the rest of the day. I knew that I was being challenged to face up to something about myself, so I committed that conversation to prayer and sat with God into the early hours of the morning, working through the issue. I was appalled at what God revealed to me. The truth is that I have been troubled by a silent anger since Clare's first diagnosis. It would not be too much of an exaggeration to say that there has been a quiet rage in my heart that needs healing so desperately. My experience of anger, along with so many others who grieve, is an experience of it as a hidden enemy. Since Clare's diagnosis and since her death, I have not had an explosive anger. I am not prone to tantrums and screaming fits. However, a seething resentment has bubbled away under the surface over the years, manifesting itself in a variety of ways.

At the beginning of Clare's illness, we would recount that story about the insensitive doctor to anyone who would listen. We would make light-hearted comments about his pastoral incompetence but, under the surface, I continued to be fuming about him and was focusing on him to express my anger at the situation in which we found ourselves. Looking back over the last few years,

I can see that my anger has been expressed in various other ways too. Leo Madow has written an excellent book called *Anger: How to Recognize and Cope With It.*[10] In it, he outlines three categories of behaviour that suggest an underlying motivating anger. The first behavioural pattern is what he calls *modified expressions of anger.* Madow suggests (p. 5) that 'these are fairly direct indications of anger but modified in form. Some are fairly open, such as "I am annoyed" or "I am irritated". Others, which we do not often think of as expressions of anger, are very revealing, such as "I am fed up", "I've had it", "I am sick and tired of that", and "I'm ready to explode".' Look below the surface of those comments and we will find anger.

The second category that Madow explores is termed *indirect expressions of anger.* As Madow notes (p. 6), 'This group is even more disguised. A most effective expression is "I am disappointed". Indirect expressions hide anger from the speaker and the listener.'

Two indirect expressions of anger that I became very used to using were 'I'm not angry, I'm just hurt, that's all', and 'That's just the way it is—I just need to get on with it'. There is a strong element of denial in such phrases that can fool even the speaker himself.

Madow calls the third category *variations of depression.* This is expressed through such phrases as 'I'm feeling a bit blue', 'I'm down in the dumps', 'There's nothing I can do about it, is there?'

Reflecting on the last eight years, I can recognize events and conversations in which I have used the phrases of all three categories but would not necessarily have attributed such responses to anger at the time. When I look below the surface, however, and analyse the context in which I have behaved in these ways, I can see that anger has indeed often been a root cause. There were times when I would claim to be 'sick and tired' of people trying to do too much for me. Conversely, I could be 'sick and tired' of the fact that nobody seemed to want to help me when I needed it. In reality, these people had not done anything wrong. Fiercely independent as I am, I was angry about my own inability to cope and my need for support. Likewise, when it became clear that some friends could not cope with the idea of supporting me through my grief and neglected to make any contact, I would think, 'I'm not angry with them—I'm just hurt, that's all.' Actually, I was seething at their insensitivity and betrayal. Furthermore, while I often congratulated myself on having survived a traumatic decade without once having to visit the doctor for medication, I often told people, 'I am feeling pretty down today', or 'I feel really tearful at the moment'. More often than not, that mild depression was triggered by a recent event or conversation that had made me feel angry and isolated in my grief.

Like many who grieve, I have not punched holes in walls in a fit of rage; nor have I become known for my irrational fits of temper. However, I stand in solidarity and commonality with the vast majority of those who have often subconsciously succumbed to a hidden enemy—the quiet rage within. This has been a most painful lesson for me to learn because I realize now the depth of my self-denial concerning this issue. I realize too the enormous amount of healing that is still needed for me to find wholeness and peace with God.

WHAT DO WE DO WITH THIS?

Having finally been confronted with such a shattering insight into the workings of my inner being, it would have been easy for me to pour guilt and condemnation upon myself. I am a Christian leader: how can it be right for me to have had such negative emotions at work in me, undetected for so many years? But the truth is that no condemnation is required because anger is not a negative emotion. Anger is a neutral emotion that can lead to either a positive or a negative pattern of behaviour. Writing to the Ephesians, Paul taught, 'If you become angry, do not let your anger lead you into sin, and do not stay angry all day' (Ephesians 4:26). It was not anger that Paul warned against. His was a warning to guard against our anger leading to something sinful. Anger itself is neither spiritually negative nor positive. It is spiritually neutral. However, anger can be utilized to bring about sinfulness or godliness in the way we respond to the event or person that creates anger within us. To that extent, then, we need not fear anger when we grieve. Rather, we need to be open and honest about our feelings, come before the throne of God with them, and allow him to use the anger within us to work for the good. That can most clearly be done with regard to the manner in which we pray during our time of grief, and the experience of the Israelites in Babylon, as recorded by the psalmist, leads us forward in our consideration of this topic.

Psalm 137 is one of the best-known passages in scripture. Ironically, though, it is well known as a result of the massive hit that Boney M had in the 1970s with their disco anthem, 'By the Rivers of Babylon'. This was an interpretation of the psalm that was popular throughout the world. It is probably not surprising, however, that when they wrote the lyrics, they decided to leave out the final two verses of Psalm 137: 'Babylon, you will be destroyed. Happy are those who pay you back for what you have done to us—who take your babies and smash them against a rock.'

These sentiments would not have been too popular on the dance floor of a 1970s discotheque. In fact, they are sentiments that are not too popular in our churches either. It is somewhat embarrassing for Christians, who are supposed to be peaceful and loving, to deal with this type of scriptural verse. It is far from easy to know what to do with a passage that appears to encourage the vicious murder of innocent children. There is such passion—such anger—in these verses. What could we possibly learn from them? Placing them in their historical context is the first step towards comprehending them and then utilizing them to guide our prayers.

This psalm was written in a period of history when the Israelites had been exiled to Babylon. The Babylonian empire was both magnificent and influential. After conquering the Assyrians, their prevailing power was felt throughout many lands. Upon attacking and conquering Israel, the people of that country were forced to relocate to Babylon itself, leaving behind their homes, possessions and businesses. All they had ever known became a distant memory. Even the temple, the ultimate symbol of their covenant relationship with God, was left in ruins.

This loss was akin to bereavement. The Israelites were in shock and in a state of grief. They were angry, and this psalm was written out of that anger. Verse 1 is so powerful in expressing that sense of loss: 'By the rivers of Babylon we sat down; there we wept when we remembered Zion.' Despite the quiet imagery of this verse, there is a deep pain being expressed. The rivers of Babylon were a series of canals built across a huge desert plain. The view that the Israelites had of these rivers would have reinforced their sense of isolation, because they were used to living in rugged terrain. They wanted desolate hills and valleys, not striking rivers and plains. The beauty of their current surroundings was no anaesthetic for the pain they felt at losing their homeland. On a number of occasions, people tried to comfort me by saying, 'Well, I'm sure you miss Clare but at least you don't have to fulfil the role of carer any more. You can relax a bit now and enjoy yourself.' For those who know the pain of loss, they would exchange any amount of exhaustion just for their partner to be alive again. The rugged hills and valleys can be more appealing than any number of rivers and plains in the right context. One person's pleasure is another person's pain.

The powerful imagery is continued in verse 2: 'On the willows near by we hung up our harps.' The Israelites had always been a people of song. The use of voice and instruments in the worship of God was part of their heritage. But now, in their pain and desolation, the harps were hung up on the willow trees. There was no noise, no playing, and no songs of rejoicing. Quite simply, they had nothing to sing about. This too is a common reaction in grief. For months after losing Clare, I simply had nothing to say to God. In my anger and depression, I did not want to use song to tell him how wonderful he was. Of course, I still believed that he was wonderful. I just had no energy or desire to put it into words. Even now, there are times when I would rather be anywhere else other than in church. The effort of worship is just too exhausting. There are times when I want to hang up my harp and go home.

The taunting of the Babylonians exacerbated the Israelites' situation. See verse 3: 'Those who captured us told us to sing; they told us to entertain them: "Sing us a song about Zion."' The reaction of God's people is entirely understandable: 'How can we sing a song to the Lord in a foreign land?' (v. 4). How could they possibly allow their praise of God to become a source of entertainment for those who did not care? For this is an important point to notice—that even in their increasing anger towards the Babylonians, the Israelites had not lost their faith. The reason they would not sing was not that they no longer trusted God to help them. It was not that they no longer believed in him. It was because their faith was so precious to them that they were not prepared to go through the motions just to keep other people happy. They were not prepared to sing and smile merely to fulfil the expectations of others.

While we may not be taunted by others in our grief, it is often the case that we are expected to 'sing a song to the Lord' when all we feel like doing is to 'hang up our harps' for a while. I found this a particular problem as a church minister: within days of Clare's death, I was expected to lead a congregation in worship and praise, and feed them with the word of God. At that stage of my life, it was a struggle to get out of bed in the morning, let alone lead others in the ways of God. Whatever position we have in the church—clergy or laity—the experience for many of us is that there is an unspoken expectation for us to worship God and play a full part in the life of the church throughout our time of grief. For most of us, there is a subconscious expectation too, as if our ability to worship is some sort of barometer of faith or a measure of our ability to cope. The feeling is that if we are not worshipping, we are somehow falling short with God and not responding as faithfully as we should. However, it is extremely harmful for us to cover up anger and hurt beneath a façade of happiness. We may please others but the inner rage will increase and eventually work itself out in unhealthier and potentially more damaging ways. The truth is that our trust in God is too important to act out in order to please or appease our fellow Christians. That is the example given to us in this psalm: 'May I never be able to play the harp again if I forget you, Jerusalem! May I never be able to sing again if I do not remember you, if I do not think of you as my greatest joy!' (vv. 5–6).

The Israelites in Babylon had a deep anger welling up inside them for many, many years. It was an anger that they could not hide from either God or themselves. It was an anger that overwhelmed them. The final three verses of the psalm are an outpouring of that anger: 'Remember, Lord, what the Edomites did the day Jerusalem was captured. Remember how they kept saying, "Tear it down to the ground!" Babylon, you will be destroyed. Happy are those who pay you back for what you have done to us—who take your babies and smash them against a rock.' We need to be honest in noting that the attitude reflected in these verses is neither godly nor pious. It is unjustifiable and sinful to wish harm upon innocent children. However, there are two vital ideas that we can take out of these verses about how to pray when we are angry.

First, we learn that true prayer is born out of passion. It is a sad truth that much of our experience in the church today is of passionless prayer. That is not an indictment of liturgical worship. It is just as easy for 'free worship' and 'open prayer' to be passionless. The form it takes does not define passionless prayer. Passionless prayer is defined by non-engagement with the issue at hand or, at best, a token engagement. God wants us to engage fully when we pray. God wants us to be passionate when we pray. He is a passionate God and he has created us in his image with passions to be expressed. Jesus' words in Revelation 3:15–16 are a damning denunciation of passionless spirituality: 'I know what you have done; I know that you are neither cold nor hot. How I wish you were either one or the other! But because you are lukewarm, neither hot nor cold, I am going to spit you out of my mouth!'

Anger is a passion that God feels and he is quite happy for us to express that in prayer. Quite simply, it is OK to show God the real force of our anger: he is big enough and strong enough to cope with it. When we are suffering the deepest anguish of grief, it is absolutely acceptable to shout and rant and rave at God. It is far better to be honest before God than to keep all the anger bottled up inside. It is easy to approach God like a hypocrite—using all the 'right' words but with a heart consumed by anger—but God is not interested in our words; he wants us to share what we really feel.

Second, and related to what we have just noted, it is quite acceptable for us to take risks when we pray passionately. The first six verses of Psalm 139 are most revealing: 'Lord, you have examined me and know me. You know everything I do; from far away you understand all my thoughts. You see me, whether I am working or resting; you know all my actions. Even before I speak, you already know what I will say. You are all round me on every side; you protect me with your power. Your knowledge of me is too deep; it is beyond my understanding.'

It seems to me that this passage is a mandate for experimentation in prayer. There are no surprises for God when we pray. He knows what we think; he knows what is in our hearts. We cannot take God by surprise. If that is the case, it is better to be upfront with God and tell him how we really feel. Intrinsic to acknowledging our anger and allowing God to heal it is the need to hand our negative emotions over to him. In order to do that, we might have to take some risks in trying new approaches to God or by saying things we are not sure are very 'godly'. What is the worst that can happen? If we pray an inappropriate prayer, or get our language wrong, or allow ourselves to be driven by a wrong motivation, it will not be the end of our relationship with God. The kingdom of heaven will not collapse! It's OK to take risks and it's OK to 'get it wrong'.

I thought that I was being very spiritual when, for several weeks, I prayed for the doctor who had treated Clare so dreadfully that fateful day in the neurological surgery. In truth, I was not concerned for him at all. I was merely using intercessory prayer to deny the fact of what I really wanted to say to God—that I hated that doctor for what he had said and the offhand way in which he had said it, and that I wanted to go back to the hospital and punch him! Now, it was not a very 'godly' emotion for me to have, but I would have been far more genuine in telling God that that was how I felt, rather than piously thanking God for the doctor and praying for his medical ministry. I was afraid to pray the truth. I was afraid of God; I was afraid of myself. I was afraid of getting it wrong. I was afraid of the overwhelming power of my anger.

Our God is a God of love. He hates to see us in any pain. He hurts when we hurt. He will do everything necessary to strengthen us and guide us through our grief. In return, we need to be honest with God about how we feel. If we can be candid about our anger and bring it to him in prayer, the way will be open for us to be healed and experience new life. I do not think it is any coincidence that, in the plan of God, Psalm 137 should be followed by Psalm 138, the first three verses of which say this: 'I thank you, Lord, with all my heart; I sing praise to you before the gods. I face your holy Temple, bow down, and praise your name because of your constant love and faithfulness, because you have shown that your name and your commands are supreme. You answered me when I called to you; with your strength you strengthened me.'

For those who are grieving, it can be a long, slow journey from the anger and bitterness of Psalm 137 to the peace of mind and sense of worship of Psalm 138. But it is a journey each one of us is called to make, not in our own strength but in the strength that God provides. When we learn to be honest with God about our anger and make the first steps towards letting go of the negativity that often grows out of it, the journey begins. The hope then is that we will be able to join the psalmist in the final verse of Psalm 138 and say to God, 'You will do everything you have promised. Lord, your love is eternal. Complete the work that you have begun.'

CHAPTER SEVEN

ACTUALLY, YOU'RE AN
OK PERSON

Ephesians 1:1-14

Even before the world was made, God had already chosen us to be his through our union with Christ, so that we would be holy and without fault before him.
EPHESIANS 1:4

Two weeks after Clare's first operation, she was able to leave hospital. It was a risky business. Her right side was extremely weak, making a wheelchair a necessity. Mobility was a real problem. Her skull was damaged from the invasive surgery and the skin on her scalp was stapled together. Headaches were still severe and she was not able to eat properly as a result of the massive bruising around her jaw.

Being the strong character that she was, though, Clare did not want to go straight home. She wanted to go for a McDonalds, since hospital food had clearly not agreed with her. So, with great trepidation, we drove to the nearest restaurant, parked up, and made the torturous journey from the car to the counter, where I placed our order. It was only then that I realized that the other customers were staring at us. Many were silent, holding their burgers midway between table and mouth. Others were whispering and laughing behind their hands. I wondered why. Then I looked at Clare and saw what they saw. My beautiful wife was barely recognizable: head half-shaven and held together with staples, face bruised and bloated from steroids; a woman tripping over her feet, body loping to one side; eyes wide, glazed and staring. Frankly, she looked pitiful. At that moment, Clare looked around her and became aware of the customers' reactions to her. She burst into tears and begged me to take her home. We slowly walked the gauntlet of suppressed laughter and made our way to the sanctuary of the car.

Of course her appearance improved rapidly. Within months, she looked as beautiful as she had always done. Nevertheless, until the day of her final admission into hospital, she was acutely aware of her physical limitations and 'inadequacies'. She was always conscious of the weakness in her right side and that she could neither walk properly nor hold a pen to write. There were many occasions on which she would trip over the paving slabs when walking down the street. Strangers would have to pick her up and, when she struggled to explain what was wrong, many suspected that she was drunk. Shopping was nearly always a humiliating experience. She could write her signature only with great difficulty and in a childish way. Customers in the queue behind her displayed their impatience at the time it was taking. Cashiers viewed her with suspicion, checking and rechecking her signature against that on the card, often calling a supervisor for clarification. Clare would have to explain her medical condition yet again and elicit the unwanted sympathy of strangers. Sadly, Clare came to hate her body and, by implication, came to dislike herself because of her limitations.

In the aftermath of Clare's death, I replayed over and over again in my mind the way in which I had cared for her. Although I knew in my heart that I had done as much as I could—and even though I knew I had done a good job over the years—all I could think of were the times I'd got it wrong. The times I had got irritated with her inability to hold an in-depth conversation. The times I had pushed her into doing things that I wanted to do when she didn't want to do them. The times when I had secretly wished her dead so that I could get on with living. In the immediate aftermath of her death, thoughts of my failings far outweighed any thoughts of how I had served Clare well in her illness. Like her, I began to dislike myself for the way I had behaved and for the thoughts I had thought.

Self-dislike, even self-hatred, is not at all unusual during the process of grief. Many of us are tortured with the phrase, 'If only...' But, of course, it's too late and we despise ourselves for the opportunities missed. In coping with this aspect of grief, we need to learn to see ourselves as God sees us. In that regard, Ephesians 1:3–14 has been a tremendously important part of my spiritual journey.

A SPIRITUAL JEKYLL AND HYDE

If we want to avoid 'self'-dislike, we need, first of all, to have some idea about what 'self' is. Philosophers throughout the ages have wrestled with this question. The most famous statement, perhaps, is Descartes' notion that 'I think, therefore I am'. However, the scriptures are categorical in the fact that the notion of 'self' is not internal but 'outward-looking'. The idea of 'self' is defined by the idea that the children of God are made in the image of God and that the purpose of our being made in his image is to know ultimate happiness. Ultimate happiness is to live in a right relationship with God. Ephesians 1 makes some extraordinary claims about our intrinsic worth as children of God:

- 'God has blessed us by giving us every spiritual blessing in the heavenly world' (v. 3).
- 'Even before the world was made, God had already chosen us to be his' (v. 4).
- 'Through Jesus Christ he would make us his sons and daughters' (v. 5).
- 'By the blood of Christ we are set free... our sins are forgiven' (v. 7).
- 'God chose us to be his own people' (v. 11).
- 'God put his stamp of ownership on you' (v. 13).

These are quite extraordinary statements. The definition of 'self' we are offered here is this: we are children of God, loved and chosen by him; we are blessed and cherished; we are forgiven; we are valued, not for what we have achieved but because of who we are. You are created in the image of God and God loves you simply because you are you.

But, of course, that is only half the story. Who and what we are is also partly defined by another event—the Fall. As well as reflecting the image of God, we also reflect the image of Adam. We are children of God but we are also children of sin. We are Jekyll and Hyde. We are mixed-up kids, holy yet depraved, beautiful yet ugly, good yet bad, saints yet sinners. We are the crowning glory of God's creation, yet we are also the filth on the bottom of the dung-heap of God's creation. We are the source of all celebration in heaven, yet we are also the reason for the crucifixion of the Son of God.

The problem with grief is this: it is such a profoundly traumatic experience that it very often leads to an imbalance in the way in which we perceive ourselves. The loss of someone close to us removes an important reference point with regard to our identity. 'Who we are' is so intertwined with our relationship with the other that when that person dies, we don't know who we are any more. Lack of clarity inevitably leads to confusion; confusion leads to imbalance; imbalance leads to negativity; negativity leads to depression; depression leads to self-hatred. The experience of grief, for so many of us, is hallmarked by dwelling on the negative aspects of our character—the bad things we did, the way we messed up, the stupid things we said. 'If only, if only, if only…' If we are to survive our grief, and use it as a creative experience through which we can grow in self-understanding and our relationship with God, we need to see ourselves differently. We need to stop defining ourselves through our experience of grief and learn to define ourselves within our relationship with God. To achieve that, we need to begin by defining ourselves in relation to the cross of Christ, because it was on a bloodstained cross on a mound of earth in a backwater part of the Roman Empire nearly 2000 years ago that our true identity was forged.

OUR IDENTITY IN CHRIST

Who we are as individuals is integrally linked to our union with Christ. Paul says as much in Romans 6:3–4: 'For surely you know that when we were baptized into union with Christ Jesus, we were baptized into union with his death. By our baptism, then, we were buried with him and shared his death, in order that, just as Christ was raised from death... so also we might live a new life.' The temptation in the aftermath of a traumatic loss is to attempt to forge a fresh start, a new way of living, by changing external circumstances—a change of social circle, decorating the house, maybe moving to a new house altogether; holidays on foreign shores, new hobbies and interests. All these things are useful and, at the right time, to be commended as a healthy part of building again during the grief process, but none of these things provides us with a new identity. Two weeks after Clare died, I flew to South Africa for the holiday of a lifetime. It was fantastic. But when I came home, I was still a grieving, broken widower. I have new friends that Clare never met, but that does not wipe out the pain of my past.

The only way to start a new life, to become a truly new creation, is in relationship to God through what he achieved for us on the cross of Calvary. Put simply, we become new people because we have died with Christ and have been raised with Christ. When Jesus died on the cross, he carried our injuries in himself so that we could be healed. When Jesus died on the cross, he carried all the anger that has eaten into our hearts, so that we could find peace. When Jesus died on the cross, he carried all that bone-weary tiredness with which grief leaves us, so that we could find rest. Free from pain, anger and tiredness, we are able, over a period of time, to become new people. This is the result of having Jesus as our substitute on the cross.

But Jesus was not just our substitute. He was our representative too. Since Jesus was representing us, we are integrally bound up with all that was achieved through his death and resurrection. Jesus represented humanity before God in his death, paying the penalty for our sin and failings. Now that penalty has been paid, it is impossible for us to live in a state of condemnation before God. The wages of sin and death have been paid to Christ and we are no longer guilty. The practical impact of that, in terms of the grief process, is that we no longer need to beat ourselves up emotionally about the way we failed the dying person, or the things we should have said but didn't, or the things we wish we could take back. As Paul wrote to the Roman church, 'Who will accuse God's chosen people? God himself declares them not guilty! Who, then, will condemn them? Not Christ Jesus, who died, or rather, who was raised to life and is at the right-hand side of God, pleading with him for us!' (Romans 8:33–34). To the Ephesians, in 1:6–8, Paul urged them to 'praise God for his glorious grace, for the free gift he gave us in his dear Son! For by the blood of Christ we are set free, that is, our sins are forgiven. How great is the grace of God, which he gave to us in such large measure!'

Through the substitutionary and representative work of Jesus Christ on the cross, we are now free from the condemnation of guilt and sin. We have been raised to new life. We are new creations. That is the reality of who we are. Our true identity is found in Christ. Of course, we may still feel a sense of regret about the past, but through the victory of Jesus Christ, the past has no power to control us or dictate the way we should live today. As Karl Barth wrote, 'I am the man of sin and this man of sin is nailed to the cross and crucified (through Jesus in my place). I am therefore destroyed and replaced...'.[11] That is the truth for each one of us as we work through our grieving process with God. The old life of sin and failure and guilt and shame has been nailed to a cross and put to death. We can now enjoy an entirely new life, founded on freedom and forgiveness.

LIVING OUT OUR IDENTITY

Philosophically or theologically, we may know that everything I have written so far is true. We know the doctrines backwards. We know what Christ achieved for us on the cross. What is more difficult, however, is to apply that knowledge into practical living. Put very simply, when we are struck down with grief, how do we live out the truth of who we are in Christ? There are, of course, no easy answers, but the way forward may lie in developing two criti-cal attitudes about ourselves: self-denial and self-affirmation. In essence, we need to deny that aspect of ourselves that has become devastated through sin and affirm that aspect of ourselves that reflects the image of God in our original creation.

Mark 8:34–35 records Jesus' challenging statement to his disciples: 'If anyone wants to come with me, he must forget self, carry his cross, and follow me. For whoever wants to save his own life will lose it; but whoever loses his life for me and for the gospel will save it.' Self-denial is not presented as an option. 'If anyone wants to come with me, *he must* forget self...' If you are not willing to do that, you cannot be a disciple of Jesus. But what does this mean?

Jesus' saying, of course, is based on the experience of crucifixion so common throughout the Roman Empire. When a condemned person was being led out to execution, they were forced to carry their own *patibulum*—the cross-beam of their cross. Jesus is there-fore making a very simple point. If we are following him with a *patibulum* on our shoulders, there is only one place we can possibly be going—out to be crucified. All that is inconsistent with the life of faith is to be put to death so that we can be raised to new life. Dietrich Bonhoeffer, a German theologian executed by the Nazis in 1944, wrote, 'When Christ calls a man, he bids him come and die.'[12] Paul, in Galatians 5:24, wrote, 'Those who belong to Christ Jesus have put to death their human nature with all its passions and desires.'

The problem with grief, though, is that it is so irrational. There are times when I feel like a new creation and then, a few hours later, I return to feeling condemned again. The mood swing can be triggered by almost anything—usually something trivial, like a song on the radio or an advert on TV or the smell of a woman's perfume as she walks past in the street, reminding me of Clare's favourite scent. The unexpected pain of a memory can be enough to trigger an irrational response of guilt in my heart. When I feel like that, I try my hardest not to feel the way I do, but the more I try, the harder it gets and the more guilt I feel at my failure to cope better. After all, a considerable period of time has passed now—surely I should be 'getting over it'!

However, what has proved so helpful to me is the realization that self-denial is not the same thing as self-achievement. Jesus has achieved it all on the cross already. There is no amount of 'effort' on my part that can make any difference at all. The whole point of self-denial is not to try to achieve a new way of living. The whole point of self-denial is to rest in the truth that a new way of living is the reality of what we already have. So Paul's statements in Ephesians 1 are always either in the past tense or speak of a present, existing reality:

- 'For in our union with Christ *he has blessed us*' (v. 3).
- 'For by the blood of Christ *we are set free*' (v. 7).
- 'God *chose us* to be his own people' (v. 11).
- 'You also *became* God's people' (v. 13).
- 'God *put* his stamp of ownership on you' (v. 13).

The truth is that I already have everything I need to forge a new life out of my experience of grief. Self-denial is not a call to me to work hard at eradicating feelings of guilt and my own sense of failure. Self-denial is a call for me to stop striving and to learn to rest in what God has already done for me in Christ. When we learn to see self-denial as a blessing rather than an unachievable sacrifice, a call to rest rather than work, it is then that we can find hope for the future in the face of grief. So it is that Paul finishes Ephesians 1:1–14, this great passage of past events and present realities, with a claim of hope for the future: 'The Spirit is the guarantee that we shall receive what God has promised his people, and this assures us that God *will give complete freedom to those who are his*. Let us praise his glory!' It is self-denial, the cessation of striving, that is the gateway to complete freedom. We are no longer guilty for our past failures—the things we failed to do, the things we wish we had an opportunity to do now. Rest in that truth and be free.

But this call to self-denial is only one side of the coin. Jesus also calls us to self-affirmation: to affirm and be confident in those aspects of ourselves that reflect the image of God. When burdened with grief and the emotions that are so often associated with grief, it is easy to forget that Jesus was actually very positive about people. We hear it in his *teaching*. Jesus said that we are more valuable than the birds and the beasts of the field. He recognized us as the crowning glory of creation. We see it in his *attitude*. Jesus despised no one. Jesus rejected no one. He went out of his way to give a sense of self-worth to those whom the world despised. He spoke courteously to women, invited little children to come and sit with him, gave hope to Samaritans and Gentiles, spent time with lepers and prostitutes and epileptics and those on the margins of society. We see it in his *activities*. Jesus acted out of compassion and a real awareness of the worth of the individual. He cried for people, he healed them and he raised them from the dead. We see it in his *death*. Jesus came not to be served but to serve. He was the Good Shepherd, laying down his life for the flock. Jesus places so much value on you and me that he was prepared to suffer and die for us.

When we look to the cross of Christ, we see the true worth of human beings. We get a real sense of our own self-worth, as Archbishop of Canterbury William Temple knew only too well: 'My worth is what I am worth to God; and that is a marvellous great deal, for Christ died for me.'[13] I read a story about a young black American boy in the 1960s suffering greatly at the hands of white racists. He put a huge banner up in his bedroom to remind himself of who he was in Christ: 'I'm me and I'm good, 'cos God don't make junk.' That is good theology. God does not make junk, but he made you and me. So actually, you're an OK person.

Grief is nearly always accompanied by regret. Certainly there are things that I would wish to change about the way I treated Clare during our marriage. But, despite our failings, we are in a position to affirm ourselves, not in a boastful manner but with grateful hearts, recognizing that God reckons us valuable and worthy. If Jesus reckons I am worth dying for, then who am I to argue? To do so is actually to make him out to be a liar.

STRIKING THE BALANCE

As Christians, we are not called to think too highly of ourselves. We are sinners before a holy and awesome God. As Paul wisely says in Romans 12:3, 'Be modest in your thinking, and judge yourself according to the amount of faith that God has given you.' Conversely, we are not called to hate ourselves. We must never think of ourselves as unlovable, unlovely and unloved. To consider ourselves unworthy of the grace of God is a gross denial of the truth about who we are and a rejection of his mercy. The process of grief is a journey through a dark valley in which shadows present as reality and perspectives get distorted. To reach the end of the valley, to become the person that the God of the valley would have you be, must begin with recognition of what is real and what is shadow. We must learn to see ourselves as God sees us—sinner yet saint, imperfect yet holy, weak yet strong, failure yet victorious.

Yes, we may have regrets. Yes, maybe there are things we would change, given a second chance. Yes, maybe there are things we should have said. Yes, maybe there are things we wish we could take back. But our identity is not forged in our past action or inactivity. Our identity was forged in the white heat of sacrificial death, on a cross, outside Jerusalem. If, in the power of the Holy Spirit, you can learn to stop striving and begin to see yourself through the eyes of God, you will come to a most profound conclusion... actually, you are an OK person.

Rest in that.

CHAPTER EIGHT

YOU'VE GOT RESPONSIBILITIES

Mark 1:40-45

'Go straight to the priest and let him examine you; then in order to prove to everyone that you are cured, offer the sacrifice that Moses ordered.'

MARK 1:44

THE COMMUNITY CONTEXT

Grief is an intensely personal experience. It was—and remains—*my* grief. There is nobody who understands how I feel. There is nobody who can experience my emotions or comprehend the depth of my pain. Ultimately, there is nobody who can dictate to me how to begin, or continue, the process of healing. It is my process; it is my grief; it is my pain.

Having said that, grief is also a community experience. I was the vicar of an East End parish when Clare died. The whole community was affected. Some 400 people attended her funeral. For the duration of the service, the school opposite the church suspended lessons and 200 children lined the pavement in silent respect. As the horse-drawn carriage moved slowly along the road, only the rhythmic clatter of the hooves on tarmac disturbed the mourning air. Walking out in front of the horses, there was a powerful realization that, although I was the chief mourner, I was far from being the only mourner. Many people were sharing in a community experience of grief that day. The loss was mine but not mine alone.

Since Clare's death, I have constantly had to remind myself of that community aspect, not just for the reason that others have suffered a loss too but also because I live in a world of complex relationships. How I feel, how I behave, how I respond to the anguish of grief, impacts on the lives of others. Conversely, how others have treated me has had a profound impact on my ability to move forward in the healing process. This chapter offers some reflections on the community aspect of grief—the responsibility of the community to the sufferer and, perhaps more importantly, vice versa. The story of the leper healed by Jesus, recorded in Mark 1:40–45, has provided some profound, if painful, insights for me in this regard.

A MOST PAINFUL EXPERIENCE

Losing both my sister and my wife was painful enough. However, the treatment I received at the hands of the church authorities throughout this period of my life was nothing short of torturous. It saddens me to have to write this chapter. This aspect of our story is one that I would rather leave buried in the past. What has prompted me to put pen to paper on this issue, though, is the fact that so many others have told me of similar episodes. Someone once said to me, 'The church is the only army that shoots its wounded.' Sadly, that seems to be the experience of too many people.

Although living under the shadow of her cancer diagnosis for nearly two years, Jackie's final decline was reasonably swift. She had enjoyed a decent period of remission after her mastectomy—nearly a year. It was Christmas week when her rapid deterioration set in and it was May when she died. During that period, Jackie received brain surgery and chemotherapy and suffered considerably. Within a short period of weeks, the brain tumours transformed her from a vibrant, energetic young mum into a shuffling, cantankerous old woman. It was heartbreaking to watch.

My bishop at the time was a good and kind man. I always considered it a privilege to serve under him. The Church of England is much the poorer for his retirement. But the truth is, he was a very busy man—a pastor too often buried under a mountain of paperwork. Nevertheless, I always looked forward to his annual visit to see me during Christmas week to bring festive greetings to my household. I was especially pleased to see him at Christmas 1998. Jackie had just had brain surgery. My friend Dave had just had his accident and was in a comatose condition. These traumas had profoundly impacted Clare and she had suffered two epileptic fits that week. As well as performing funerals, attending various local nativity activities and sorting out the Christmas services, I was trying to look after Clare and Rebekah in between travelling nearly one hundred miles a day to visit my friend and my sister in their respective hospitals.

When the bishop arrived, I told him the situation in which I found myself. He sat quietly as I talked but was clearly distracted. After half an hour, he got up to leave. 'Well,' he said, 'have a really good Christmas.' I was stunned. The bishop had listened but not heard.

Early in January, I had cause to meet with the archdeacon to discuss a major church refurbishment project we had recently completed. I outlined to him my circumstances and he listened sympathetically. Thereafter, I heard nothing from those in authority over me.

Jackie died on Thursday. Although informed of my loss, my superiors did not contact me. Indeed, I had to lead the service on the Sunday after her death and was never offered compassionate leave. I took a day off to perform Jackie's funeral but then was expected to carry on as if nothing had happened. At my annual performance review, I poured out my anger and sense of hurt concerning this oversight. The archdeacon conceded that a pastoral error had been made and that it should not happen again.

A few months after my review, in January 2001, Clare collapsed while I was teaching in India. She was immediately admitted to hospital and underwent further radical brain surgery. The bishop visited her in hospital and we were grateful for that caring act. However, from the day she left hospital in January until the day she died in July, Clare received neither a visit nor a card nor a phone call from any of my ecclesiastical superiors. She was stunned and hurt that she should have to suffer so much, and face her impending death, without the spiritual care of the Church. When she died, she was strong in the faith of Jesus Christ, but any respect she had for the institution she had served so tirelessly was absolutely shattered. Quite simply, she felt betrayed.

I found it beyond comprehension that, the week Clare was dying, those in spiritual authority over us did not help out with arrangements for the impending Sunday worship at our church. I was required to do that by phone from my dying wife's bedside. A layman in the congregation was expected to conduct the service, break the news of Clare's death and lead the community in grief: no rural dean or archdeacon or bishop could free themselves from previous commitments. Understandably, the layman was extremely apprehensive about this task and I had to be a pastoral support for him in that situation when I barely had enough spiritual resources to cope myself.

Then Clare died. The bishop visited me in hospital and we prayed alongside her body. He offered to give the sermon at Clare's funeral and was extremely supportive and sensitive in that regard. However, I was not contacted by any other member of the clergy at that time. More amazing still, I was not offered any compassionate leave. I had to continue with my ministry as if nothing had happened. Within ten days of Clare's death, I had performed the Sunday services, led a funeral and was undertaking marriage preparation for a young couple in the parish, as well as all the other administrative tasks involved in parochial ministry.

I was feeling hurt and betrayed by this treatment and wrote a letter to the diocesan bishop outlining my grievance. In his reply, he noted that I obviously had a lot of anger in me following Clare's death and that he would pray for me.

I was angry at the church authorities. I felt that I had been the recipient of gross pastoral misconduct, not once but twice. There was no way in which the past could be undone for me, but I was concerned that no other minister should have to endure such dreadful treatment. I requested a meeting with my local bishop, archdeacon and rural dean to outline my grievance, and implored them to set in place the structures that would prevent it from happening again. It took thirteen letters, six e-mails and five phone calls over a period of two months before they would agree to meet with me.

I realized that I had a choice: I could seek some form of retribution for the manner in which I had been treated or I could forgive them. I struggled greatly with this because there was so much anger inside. I prayed tirelessly, and instinctively knew what I should do. At the meeting, I read out a three-page statement, outlining the course of events and how I felt. We talked the issues through and sought to be reconciled to each other. Thereafter, I forgave them for hurting me so badly and never mentioned the matter again.

It would have been easier for me to remain on the margins of the community, consumed by anger and bitterness. I could have left the ministry or, more damaging still, remained a vicar with a twisted and bitter heart. I believe, however, that by confronting the authorities with the truth, the way was cleared for us all to accept our responsibilities and receive the corporate healing that was so desperately needed. It is to their credit that, when a local minister developed a brain tumour within two months of this episode, they offered extraordinary pastoral support to him and did all they could to make his death a peaceful one. They had learnt their responsibilities in pastoral care. I had learnt how to forgive. We could be reconciled as brothers and sisters once more.

LIVING ON THE MARGINS

It is almost impossible to define the nature of the man's illness in Mark 1:40–45. To be sure, he is called a leper but the Greek term *lepros* speaks of at least three forms of leprosy and various other skin diseases common in Jesus' time. First, there was nodular leprosy or tubercular leprosy. This was recognizable by brown nodules forming on discoloured patches of skin, primarily around the cheek, nose, lips and forehead. Thereafter, ulceration occurred —both on those nodules and on the hands, feet and other parts of the body. Finally, mental illness and coma would precede death.

Second, there was anaesthetic leprosy, a condition that could be endured for thirty years or more. This was similar in terms of symptoms but with the added trauma of a seriously affected nervous system. The victim would lose all sensation in hands and feet and would therefore be susceptible to burns and infections. Muscles would deteriorate and it would not be unusual for the feet either to drop off or to waste away completely.

The third form was a mixture of tubercular and anaesthetic leprosy. This was probably the most common at the time and is described in Leviticus 13. However, that passage also makes clear that a number of other skin diseases were considered to make a person 'unclean'. Not all cases led to this socially stigmatic pronouncement. There were four tests for uncleanness. The skin disease had to be older than one week, it had to go deeper than the first layer of skin, it had to be irremovable by washing and it had to be patchy, affecting only part of the person. It is likely that skin conditions such as eczema or psoriasis would have fallen within the category denoted by the term *lepros*.

While it is impossible to state with any certainty the exact nature of the man's illness in Mark 1, it is abundantly clear that he was, and had been for some time, declared ritually and ceremonially unclean. He was ostracized from society, living out his days on the margins, prevented from entering the holy city of Jerusalem. He was condemned to a life on his own, or living with other outcasts. He would have been required to shave his head and wear torn clothes. If he ever came into contact with others, he was required to warn of his presence by shouting, 'Unclean! Unclean!' Many would have believed that the ill fortune that had befallen him was a result of serious sin—that his sickness was some form of divine punishment. Perhaps he believed that about himself.

The courage of the man in Mark's account is not in doubt. In verse 40, we read that he 'came to Jesus, knelt down and begged him for help'. As a social outcast, it would have been easier for him to hide in the hills and watch Jesus walk by. This man was hurting enough, emotionally and physically. To come out from the rocks with such vulnerability and with such a display of humiliation demanded great strength of character. It cost him dearly to 'come, kneel, beg'. That he thought so little of himself is evident in his request to Jesus (v. 40). He does not say, 'If you *can*...' but 'If you *want to*...' There is no doubt in his mind about Jesus' ability to heal. The question is, why would Jesus want to waste his energy on such a pathetic human as this?

Jesus responded to this man by being 'filled with pity' (v. 41). The Greek word that describes this emotion is *orgistheis*, which expresses the notion of being angry. But Jesus' anger was not the same as that which the man had encountered in the past. Jesus was not angry with the man for being such a sinner. Jesus was not angry with him for being a social embarrassment. Jesus was not angry with him for being so visibly 'unclean'. Jesus was angry that one of God's children should have become so disfigured and marred by sickness. The very existence of sickness and disease—the notion that any one of his precious creatures should be in pain—filled him with righteous anger. Furthermore, Jesus was filled with righteous anger about a system and a society that should force those who hurt the most on to its very margins, where they could be ignored or even forgotten completely.

There is real power in verse 41. 'Jesus... stretched out his hand and touched him.' Perhaps you remember the astonishment and wonder when Princess Diana visited a hospitalized AIDS patient soon after the illness had first become recognized. She sat beside his bed and gently laid her gloveless hand upon his. It was the power of touch—the ultimate symbol of social acceptability—that did so much to confront society with its own ignorance and bigotry. The impact of Jesus touching a leper would have been much the same. But then Jesus went on to do what no mere mortal could. He declared the reality of healing and 'at once the disease left the man' (v. 42).

Jesus' action thereafter initially seems somewhat puzzling. 'Then Jesus spoke sternly to him and sent him away at once, after saying to him, "Listen, don't tell anyone about this"' (vv. 43–44). The strength of Jesus' command is not in doubt. First, he 'spoke sternly'. Second, in saying, 'Don't tell anyone about this', he used a double negative to express the seriousness of his intention: *medeni meden eipes*. Why should he have wanted the healed man to keep quiet? There are many theories concerning Mark's repeated idea of Jesus requesting secrecy in his ministry (compare 1:34; 3:12; 5:43; 7:36; 8:30; 9:9)—what has become known as the 'messianic secret'. It is not for us to explore those theories here. What I found so challenging in reading this passage was the notion that Jesus was intent on providing holistic healing rather than merely partial healing. To be sure, he dealt quickly with the physical symptoms of disease by ridding the man of his leprosy. To the observer, the healing was then complete. However, Jesus was acutely aware of the wider need for healing—that the man now had to be reintegrated into society. It was no longer appropriate for him to stay on the margins. He had to take his rightful place in the community. For the reason that his healing was thus far only partial, Jesus commanded him to remain quiet until he had seen the priest, been declared clean and offered his Mosaic sacrifice (v. 44).

Yet the onus was on the man to go back. Even though he had been sinned against through the ignorance and prejudice of the community, Jesus expected the man to make the first move towards reconciliation. In the circumstances, there was a real sacrifice expected of him. Not only had he 'come, knelt, begged' before Jesus, but now he was required to walk through the streets under the suspicious gaze of the inhabitants and present himself for examination by the priest. This was no private event. According to Leviticus 14, he would have been examined once before a sacrifice of a bird was made. Cedar, scarlet, hyssop and a live bird would then be taken and dipped in the blood of the dead bird. Thereafter, the healed man would have washed and shaved himself completely. Seven days later, he would have been subjected to a second examination. Another complete shave was required before making a sacrifice of lambs, flour and oil. A third examination was required before the priest would issue a certificate making a public declaration of the cleansing.

This process inevitably demanded strength of character and a deep sense of humility. A lesser person would have baulked at the idea of subjecting himself to such public scrutiny: 'I am the victim here! The community of believers have treated me dreadfully. They didn't stand by me when I was hurting. They just pushed me out on to the margins where they wouldn't have to see me or even think about me. Sure, some of them threw me bread occasionally and told me they were praying for me. But that was just to make them feel better about themselves. When I was in real pain, they did not stand by me. Why can't the priest come out to me? Why do I have to go to him? Why can't someone come and apologize for the way they've treated me? It's just not fair!'

The man did not go straight to the priest. In verse 45, we are told that he 'went away and began to spread the news everywhere'. One cannot blame him for getting carried away in his excitement at having received physical healing. Perhaps, having met with the living Christ in such a personal and powerful way, he needed some space and time before re-establishing a relationship with the religious institution. In all likelihood, though, he would have visited the priest soon after and made his sacrifice, otherwise he would have remained an outcast. Whatever the time span or chronology of events, it is clear that his reintegration into society began that day.

THE RESPONSIBILITY TO FORGIVE AND RECONCILE

'Blessed are those who mourn, for they shall be comforted' (Matthew 5:4, RSV). That is the mandate of God for those who hurt. Sadly, however, it is not always the experience of those who turn to the Church for solace. Too often, those who are recently bereaved or divorced, or who may be traumatized by having chosen a termination or through facing some other major crisis, are the subject of unspoken judgment. Still others must endure open and hostile criticism. More often than not, this is directed towards Christians who, although they have devoted their life to the Church, are seen now as moral failures. Sometimes, the deprivation of comfort is less harsh than that but just as damaging. This is particularly the case with the bereaved, who may be well supported in the initial stages of grief but, after six months or so, find themselves passed over for the next 'needy case' that has come along. By the time we have to face our first Christmas alone, our first birthday alone, the first re-run of that series our partner loved so much, our first summer day, our first snowfall alone, the Christian community seems to have moved on. We are left alone and comfortless—and it hurts.

The hard truth, though, is that God requires us to be proactive. As we begin to receive his healing and start the process of re-building, so we have a responsibility to recognize, and grapple with, the corporate dimension of our renewal. If we have been hurt or feel rejected by the Christian community, it is easy to remain on the margins, lost in self-pity and isolated consolation. However, that is not the way of Christ. His example to us is one of self-giving, vulnerability and humility. Just as Jesus Christ constantly sought out and lived among a community that misunderstood him, despised him and rejected him, so we too are called to seek out our brothers and sisters in the faith and live with them. Just as Jesus Christ forgave those who had hurt him, so we are called to forgive those who have hurt us. Just as Jesus Christ took his brokenness and used it in ministry for others who hurt, so we too must follow that example and use the reality of who we are—who we have become—to bring glory to God and comfort to the broken-hearted.

There are many times in my own ministry when I have had the privilege of praying with people for their healing. Often this has

been with those seeking relief from the effects of arthritis that has
gnarled their hand into a tight ball. Sometimes I have prayed with
those suffering from an unsightly skin condition or constant
headaches. More often than not, I have found that accompanying
(though by no means always causing) such conditions has been a
bitterness of heart—unwillingness or an inability to forgive someone who has caused pain in the past. As we have prayed that issue
through, and the person has made the conscious decision to
forgive, so a deep healing has taken place. The bitterness of heart
disappears and with it goes the arthritic hand or the skin complaint
or the headaches.

In his *Devotions*, John Donne famously noted, 'No man is an
Island, entire of it self.' This is not just an astute observation. It is
good theology. We have been created in the image of a triune God—
Father, Son and Holy Spirit. There is community and relationship
at the very heart of the being of God. Indeed, community and
relationship are the very definition of God. If we are to reflect that
image fully, so we need to find our place within community and
within restored and fully reconciled relationships. Our destiny as
children of God is to find our place within the community of God.
If the community has encouraged us, we take our sense of joy and
give it back for the benefit of that community. If the community has
hurt us, we take our pain and are open about it, and forgive so that
the community may learn and be strengthened for the future. Isolation is not an option. Withdrawal is not an option. That is not the
way of Christ. Our way is to follow the one who taught that 'the Son
of Man did not come to be served; he came to serve and to give his
life to redeem many people' (Mark 10:45).

If we can be strong in character, faith and obedience and return
to the community of faith after having been misunderstood or
rejected, something wonderful will happen. On a personal level, we
will receive a depth of healing and peace beyond our imagination.
We will return as prophets, speaking from our experience on the
margins, giving voice to the voiceless. Finally, the community itself
will be forced to confront its own fallibility and, if it is willing to

undergo a process of introspective examination and repentance, will be strengthened in its ministry and in its witness for God. My favourite portion of scripture is Ephesians 1:19–20: 'This power working in us is the same as the mighty strength which he used when he raised Christ from death and seated him at his right side in the heavenly world.' God is working resurrection power in our lives and in our Christian communities, but first, we must be willing to lay down our lives and die if we want to be raised. The challenge for us personally is to lay down our pride and be proactive in seeking forgiveness and reconciliation. The challenge to the community is to acknowledge its sin, to accept forgiveness and to learn for the future.

Utilizing pain can be prophetic. If you have been hurt, you are called to be a prophet. Do not despise that calling. Like the man in Mark 1:40–45, take up your responsibility, go back to the Christian community from which you have become marginalized and begin again to offer the sacrifice of worship, praise and ministry. Do not be afraid to follow his example and 'spread the news everywhere'. If you have been healed, you have a story to tell. The world is waiting to hear it. The world is waiting to respond to the glorious healing grace of God.

CHAPTER NINE

BACK TO THE LIGHT AGAIN

Jonah 2

'When I felt my life slipping away, then, O Lord, I prayed to you, and in your holy Temple you heard me.'
JONAH 2:7

SEAWEED AROUND MY HEAD

It was six o'clock in the morning. I woke up awkwardly on my mattress, lying on the floor at the foot of Clare's hospital bed. I had been keeping my vigil for seven days now and was becoming used to the morning ritual. However, reaching up to hold her hand, I was immediately startled by how cold and clammy Clare was. Her breathing had become very shallow. Her throat was rattling. This morning, the ritual would be very different. I knew what was happening and I felt dizzy and sick.

I sat down on the chair, kissed Clare gently on the lips and reached for my Bible. For the next hour, I read aloud to her from the scriptures, focusing especially on our favourite passages. I sang her favourite hymns and Christian songs. I talked to her and said all I wanted to say—all I needed to say; all she needed to hear. I prayed with her and for her. I cried with her and for her. I cried for Rebekah. I cried for me.

I phoned Clare's mum and dad and, within half an hour, they arrived. I left them alone with their precious little girl. I do not know the details of their time together. It is not for me to know.

After an hour, I returned and sat beside Clare. We all prayed together and, as I stroked Clare's hair, I told her it was time for her to go home. We would be OK. We would look after Rebekah. I thanked her for a most wonderful marriage and, as her breathing became more laboured, I gave her a blessing and commended her into the loving arms of God. I stroked her forehead and said, 'Goodbye, my angel.'

And then my darling wife was gone.

Gone.

No longer alive.

Dead.

It was as if someone had torn open my chest, ripped out my heart and was stamping it into the ground. I have never before or since felt such an intense pain. Red-hot pokers searing into my brain. Dizziness. Sickness. I wanted to scream and scream and scream and scream—not in frenzy but in an attempt to release the sheer agony that was racking my body. But I did not scream. I was silent.

I walked out of the room, found a nurse and informed her that Clare had died. I walked down the corridor, down the stairs and out on to the bustling London street. It was 9.15am. Commuters rushed past me on their way to work. Cars hooted through congestion-induced frustration. But I was living in a parallel world, observing the normality around me, yet completely disconnected. There was a loud buzzing in my ears, my head was filled with white noise. I was confused and dazed.

It was a feeling that stayed with me, with greater or lesser intensity, for many weeks. Even now, a year after Clare's death, I still have regular episodes of confusion. My mind cannot focus. I feel tearful. Group dynamics and multi-person conversations leave me feeling dazed. I cannot describe this fearful sensation any better than Jonah did in his prayer: 'The water came over me and choked me; the sea covered me completely, and seaweed was wrapped around my head' (v. 5). What a marvellous analogy. The claustrophobic sensation of having my head smothered with clinging, slimy, suffocating seaweed is exactly how I felt. It perfectly describes how I so often feel even now. Jonah 2 is a chapter that has been immensely helpful in my own journey through the grieving process—ironic, maybe, since the book of Jonah was Clare's favourite portion of scripture.

JONAH'S PREDICAMENT

The story of Jonah is one of the most vivid in the Bible. His predicament, his emotions, his humanity are portrayed with stark reality: we are able to picture the scene so clearly. As with all good stories, however, there is a power in what is not said as well as what is. We are invited by the writer to use our imagination to feel the full force of events.

We can imagine the scene as the storm lashes the ship. We can imagine the sailors desperately trying to save the vessel and their own lives—frantic activity, shouts of command being lost in the howling wind, fear and anxiety, prayers being offered in utter desperation. They are men of compassion as well as men of strength. Jonah confesses to being the reason for the curse but they do not want to sacrifice his life to save their own. They struggle in vain to row their way out of the tempest. Finally, they are forced to throw Jonah overboard and throw themselves on the mercy of God.

All becomes still.

For the sailors, there is the stillness of calm after the storm. The waves cease their buffeting, the wind quietens and, in silent relief and with thanksgiving, these men of the sea make their way home, chastened by events.

For Jonah, however, the stillness is very different. From the noise and activity of the storm, he plummets into the waves and encounters the eerie calm that is found beneath the surface of water. He sinks slowly into the darkness, aware that his life will soon be lost and that he is destined to remain for ever captive to this silent, watery grave. Jonah feels utterly alone, cocooned in his own fear. There is silence as he sinks.

For those who know the pain of grief, the silence of suffering is to be greatly feared. There are simply no words to describe the pain inside. No matter how compassionate or wise others may be, they simply do not understand what you are going through. How can they know when they cannot feel your pain? They may have had similar experiences, but your pain is your own—uniquely your own. To be sure, we can talk to others about how we feel and benefit from that, but there comes a moment when words are inadequate to describe the deep-seated agony and we are thrown back on to the realization that God alone can be Counsellor and Healer.

THE GRACE OF GOD

The grace of God can be at work in our lives often in the strangest of ways. I received wise advice from a work colleague during the early period of my loss. We were talking about the various stages of the bereavement process as outlined by Elisabeth Kubler-Ross in *On Death and Dying*—denial, anger, bargaining, depression and acceptance.[14] My colleague noted that the denial stage was actually highly beneficial in that it is nature's way of cushioning the shock of loss. He said, 'If I were you, I would stay in the denial stage for as long as you can. There will be plenty of time to deal with your pain throughout the rest of your life.'

This was a completely different way of seeing things. For me, the denial stage was to be rushed through because I felt guilty at not wanting to face the reality of what had happened. I saw the denial stage as a curse and not a blessing, an enemy and not a friend. I felt that to be lost in denial was a sign of weakness. I believed that I had to get a grip on reality if I was to move forward with myself and with God. However, my colleague led me to understand denial as a gift from God and not a spiritual blockage. As an act of grace, God conditions the human psyche to enter into denial until such time as it is ready to begin the process of healing. For some, that is a brief

period. For others, it may last months or even years. However long
it lasts, the denial stage is a friend and not an enemy. It is a gift from
our gracious God.

This realization led me to re-examine the role of the large fish
that swallowed Jonah. I had always thought of this as the ultimate
disaster to strike him. Not only had Jonah been thrown overboard,
not only was he sinking—now he was being eaten by a fish. But
then I read 1:17 again: 'At the Lord's command a large fish
swallowed Jonah.' Yes, *at the Lord's command*. In a bizarre way, the
presence and activity of the fish was an act of grace on behalf of
God. If the fish had not swallowed Jonah, he would have drowned.
The fish was sent by God to save Jonah's life. Even though it must
have felt to him as if things could not get any worse, Jonah was
actually experiencing the ironic grace of God.

It can be the worst of clichés to say that 'God works in mysterious ways', but when he offers us grace, it is very true.

Jonah spent three days and nights inside the belly of the fish—
plenty of time to sit and reflect on what was and what had been. In
coming to terms with this life-shattering trauma, Jonah prayed. He
began with remembrance of his positive experience of God in the
past and ended with hope for the future. He was wise to do this,
since perspective on our present predicament can be gained only
within that context of past experience and future hope. As we come
now to study Jonah's prayer in some depth, there are six primary
ideas upon which we can draw in order to gain a true perspective
on our own experience of grief and suffering.

THE IMPORTANCE OF SCRIPTURE

Jonah based his prayer on the Psalms. The words and ideas he used
were not random. Nor were they casually thrown together. In lifting
his voice to God, Jonah drew on the rich spiritual tradition of his
forefathers. Here are some comparative examples.

In my distress, O Lord, I called to you, and you answered me.
JONAH 2:2

When I was in trouble, I called to the Lord, and he answered me.
PSALM 120:1

From deep in the world of the dead I cried for help, and you heard me.
JONAH 2:2

I cried to you for help, O Lord my God… you kept me from the grave. I was on my way to the depths below, but you restored my life.
PSALM 30:2–3

The waters were all round me, and all your mighty waves rolled over me.
JONAH 2:3:

I am in deep water, and the waves are about to drown me.
PSALM 69:2

He has sent waves of sorrow over my soul.
PSALM 42:6

I thought I had been banished from your presence.
JONAH 2:4

I was afraid and thought that he had driven me out of his presence.
PSALM 31:22

The water closed in over me, the deep was round about me.
JONAH 2:5 (RSV)

The danger of death was all round me; the waves of destruction rolled over me.
PSALM 18:4

But you, O Lord my God, brought me back from the depths alive.
JONAH 2:6

He keeps me from the grave and blesses me with love and mercy.
PSALM 103:4

When I felt my life slipping away, then, O Lord, I prayed to you.
JONAH 2:7

*So I am ready to give up; I am in deep despair. I remember the days gone
by… I lift up my hands to you in prayer.*
PSALM 143:4–6

I prayed to you, and in your holy Temple you heard me.
JONAH 2:7

*In my trouble I called to the Lord; I called to my God for help. In his
temple he heard my voice; he listened to my cry for help.*
PSALM 18:6

Those who worship worthless idols have abandoned their loyalty to you.
JONAH 2:8

You hate those who worship false gods, but I trust in you.
PSALM 31:6

*But I will sing praises to you; I will offer you a sacrifice and do what I have
promised.*
JONAH 2:9

I will give you a sacrifice of thanksgiving and offer my prayer to you.
PSALM 116:17

*In the full assembly I will praise you for what you have done; in the
presence of those who worship you I will offer the sacrifices I promised.*
PSALM 22:25

Salvation comes from the Lord!
JONAH 2:9

Victory comes from the Lord.
PSALM 3:8

In 1987, the Archbishop of Canterbury's Envoy Terry Waite went to Beirut to negotiate for the release of several Western hostages. He was kidnapped and taken hostage himself, remaining in captivity for 1760 days, the first four years of which he endured in solitary confinement. His story is told in *Taken on Trust*[15]—an extraordinary account of a situation that tested both his own endurance and the strength of the human spirit. Waite has noted that his knowledge of the scriptures and the *Book of Common Prayer* often provided the resources he needed to retain his faith in God and his hope of deliverance. Terry Waite knew his Bible and, when he was inside the metaphorical fish-belly, blindfolded and chained to a wall, he was able to draw comfort from the word of God.

Grief is incredibly tiring. Energy is sapped. Very often, the last thing we want to do is sit down to read a book—even the Bible. It is at these times that the importance of knowing the promises of God in scripture is so important.

THE DEPTHS OF GRACE

In verse 2, we read Jonah's words, 'From deep in the world of the dead I cried for help, and you heard me.' Jonah was in absolute despair when he called out to God. He felt completely cut off from his Lord—beyond salvation. How could God possibly hear him in the belly of a fish in the depths of the ocean? Yet God did hear his prayer and brought him redemption. The reality of grief is that nobody truly understands and that, no matter how much we share about how we feel, nobody can comprehend the depths of our pain and sense of isolation. But God hears and God understands. There is nowhere too far away from God. Regardless of how we may feel, there is always the hope that we shall be heard and that we shall be healed.

THE SOVEREIGNTY OF GOD

I have written much about the sovereignty of God in Chapter One and do not want to repeat it here. However, it is pertinent to consider Jonah's prayerful words, recorded in verse 3: 'You threw me down into the depths, to the very bottom of the sea, where the waters were all around me, and all your mighty waves rolled over me.' This is not to say that God was responsible for Jonah's dilemma. It was not God who had made him run away and set sail on that ship. It was not God who inspired the sailors to throw him overboard. Once Jonah was in the sea, however, God heard his cry and 'threw [him] down to the depths, to the very bottom of the sea, where the waters were all around...' and where the fish was waiting for him. God was not the instigator of the disaster but his sovereignty overruled, and preserved Jonah's life. Of course, Jonah did not perceive the events as such at the time: 'I thought I had been banished from your presence' (v. 4), but the sovereignty of God was clearly understood in retrospect, which is so often the case in the grieving process.

THE LOWEST POINT

Two months after Clare died, my daughter Rebekah had gone away for a brief break with my parents. I was on my own for the evening and was feeling very depressed. Obviously, it wasn't the first time I had felt that way but, for some reason, that evening the pain was more acute. Foolishly in retrospect, I chose that night to watch my wedding video and sort through some photographs that had lain in a drawer for too long. Eventually, I lay on the sofa with a bottle of Jack Daniel's whiskey, and reminisced. The phone rang—five, maybe six times—and each time I ignored it. Before I knew it, the bottle was empty, it was three o'clock in the morning and I was on the floor in tears, arms wrapped around my chest, rocking gently in pain. At that moment, I realized just how serious was the situation in which I found myself. I was grieving. I was depressed. As the weeks had passed, I was drinking more and more heavily. I was cutting myself off from my friends and family. I could not see any future. I felt absolutely hopeless. I was at the lowest point in my life. I realized that, if I did not do something positive to remedy the situation, I would suffer a nervous breakdown or worse. From there on in, I began the long, slow process of rebuilding my life— a process that continues even now. However, I had had to reach that lowest point in order to recognize the seriousness of my situation.

The prodigal son had to live and work among the pigs before he came to his senses and decided to return to his father (Luke 15:16–17). Likewise, Jonah had to be in the belly of the fish, feeling utterly desolate before he decided to 'look again toward Thy holy temple' (v. 4, NASB). It is so very, very painful to hit that low point during the grieving process, but it is a necessary point to reach if we are to return to our Father. We can receive grace only when we become aware of how desperately we are in need of grace. When we hit the lowest point, and recognize our need of God, the only suitable response is to join with Jonah: 'When I felt my life slipping away, then, O Lord, I prayed to you, and in your holy Temple you heard me' (v. 7). In all likelihood, prayer is the last activity in which we feel like engaging. It is, however, essential. The prayers do not have to be long. We do not need to impress God with our eloquent reflections. It was John Bunyan who once said, 'The best prayers are more often groans than words.'[16] It is enough, when we reach our lowest point, to cry out, 'Lord, have mercy.' And he will.

DESPERATE IDOLATRY

From the moment of her original diagnosis, I prayed for Clare's healing every single day. There was nothing I wanted more. I would have given anything—even my own life—for her to be well again. I prayed and I prayed and I prayed and I prayed. But each six-monthly brain scan revealed the awful truth that matters were getting worse, not better.

I began to believe that my prayer methodology was at fault. If only I could pray properly, Clare would be healed. So I began to experiment with different ways of praying. I begged God to heal her. I demanded that God heal her. I claimed healing in the name of Jesus Christ. I claimed the victory of the cross over the power of Satan in this situation. I bartered with him. I bargained with him. When these 'methods' did not work, I tried alternative approaches. I prayed silently. I prayed in tongues. I prayed to the Virgin Mary. I prayed to as many saints as I could remember. After my sister died, I prayed to her, imploring her to intervene. I prayed on my knees, I prayed sitting down, I prayed standing up, I prayed prostrate on the floor. I prayed in the words of scripture, I prayed in my own words.

Clare was not healed. Despite my prayers, she died.

When I reflect on my foolish attempts to 'pray appropriately', I am chastened by Jonah's words in verse 8: 'Those who worship worthless idols have abandoned their loyalty to you.' Retrospectively, it is clear that I turned prayer into an idol. I was more concerned about my strategy, my methodology—getting it right—than I was about the God to whom I was praying. I treated prayer as some sort of magic formula rather than marvellous friendship, incantation rather than conversation—worthless idolatry, as if God could be bought or impressed into action by my spectacular spirituality.

In retrospect, too, I am quite clear that my idolatrous praying was no barrier to Clare's healing. Not for one moment do I believe that if I had 'got it right', she would have lived. God's grace is far bigger than that. He is not dependent on us. I was the only loser in this situation because I was living with a false perception of God. Perhaps I would have known a greater degree of peace if I had surrendered the situation to him at an earlier stage. Perhaps I would have handled the trauma better than I did. But I did not—and that's OK. It is OK to make mistakes. It is OK to get it wrong. It is OK, in the mind-numbing confusion and agony of grief and suffering, to be inappropriate with God. What is the worst that can happen? We might have to say sorry and reassess. God is big enough. He can handle that.

BACK TO THE LIGHT AGAIN

From deep within the belly of the fish, Jonah remembers, reflects and refocuses. At the lowest point of his life, he becomes deeply impacted by the ironic, generous, overwhelming grace of God. His prayer is nothing less than a spiritual journey—from despair to devotion. As he finally comprehends the profound love God has for him, Jonah dedicates himself back to his service: 'But I will sing praises to you; I will offer you a sacrifice and do what I have promised. Salvation comes from the Lord!' (v. 9).

What is so amazing is that Jonah utters these words while still in the belly of the fish. He does not barter with God: 'If you get me out of this mess, I will sing praises to you...' As far as Jonah knows, there is no escape from his predicament. He will see out his final hours there, after which his corpse will be lost to the watery depths. Jonah had reached a level of great spiritual wisdom and maturity in which he no longer equated salvation with deliverance from his dilemma. Jonah had realized that salvation is about having a relationship with God. Salvation can occur even in the darkest of times. That is why I get so irritated when people comment that Clare lost her battle against cancer. No, she did not. She won the battle because not even cancer could rob her of salvation. Experiencing the peace of God that passes all understanding is absolutely dependent on this.

Jonah cried out with conviction and passion, 'Salvation comes from the Lord!' It is no surprise what comes next: 'Then the Lord ordered the fish to spew Jonah up on the beach, and it did' (v. 10). The spewing out of Jonah after three days seems to be a prophetic scripture, pointing to the resurrection of Jesus. But the experience of resurrection is one that is available to us all—and not only after death. Resurrection is a way of living. Resurrection can be a daily experience. When we can join with Jonah and cry out, 'Salvation comes from the Lord!'—even when we are trapped in the belly of whatever crisis has swallowed us—then we can know the power of resurrection that will sustain us and give us the ability to face whatever tomorrow may bring.

CHAPTER TEN

MISSION POSSIBLE

John 21:15-19

After they had eaten, Jesus said to Simon Peter, 'Simon, son of John, do you love me more than these others do?'

'Yes, Lord,' he answered, 'you know that I love you.'

JOHN 21:15

RUNNING ON EMPTY

It was Sunday morning. Clare had been dead three months. I did not need the alarm clock to wake me these days. I was regularly going to bed at two o'clock in the morning and waking up at five o'clock. During the week, I would get up and do some housework. On Sundays, however, I would stay in bed because it had become the one day of the week when I did not want to get up. It was the day when I would have to go to church, lead the congregation in worship and minister to their spiritual needs. While I still loved the congregation dearly and felt confident in administering the Eucharist, I was finding it increasingly difficult to preach from the word of God. It was not that I no longer believed the good news. It was just that I was so very tired and the thought of preparing and delivering an inspiring message week on week was becoming increasingly difficult. But this particular Sunday was different for the reason that I had finally reached the end of my tether. For the first time in ten years of my ordained ministry, I went into church with no sermon prepared. For the first time in ten years of my

117

ordained ministry, I could not have cared less. I was physically, spiritually and emotionally exhausted. The service started and I was in a daze as the worship leader fulfilled his responsibilities. Hymns, liturgy and readings came and went. I heard nothing. Eventually, it was time for the sermon. I moved gingerly to the lectern and leant upon it. I looked out at the congregation. My gaze moved slowly round the church. I said nothing for a minute or so. The parishioners looked back at me. Some shuffled in their seats, uncomfortable in the silence. Eventually, after what seemed like an age, I spoke in a monotonous tone.

'I am so tired. I have absolutely nothing to say to you today. I'm sorry.'

I moved back to my seat and sat down. There was stunned silence. Nobody quite knew what to do next. Eventually, the person leading the prayers came to the front and the service continued according to plan, according to tradition. Following the service, a number of parishioners avoided me but one or two others hugged me, told me they loved me and that they would continue to pray for me. That was the response I needed after having made myself so terribly vulnerable.

A few months later, I was visiting South Africa to attend a youth ministry conference and chair a session there. I had the pleasure of staying with some close friends in Durban. One morning, enjoying breakfast on the sun-soaked beach with Keith, I was pouring out my heart about how I was feeling and the struggle of working through the grieving process. I related to him the events of that Sunday morning and how desperate I had felt. I was close to tears and, for the first time, vocalized the awful truth that had been eating away at me.

'Keith, I have nothing left to give any more. I think my ministry is over.'

Keith is an immensely wise man. God is at work so powerfully in him and through him that I always respect what he has to say. However, I was completely unprepared for his next comment.

'What do you mean?' he asked gently. 'Your ministry is far from over! Why aren't you writing a book about your experiences?'

I could not believe it. 'Don't be silly,' I replied, 'I haven't got a story to tell. I've got a series of fractured images, mostly related to how much I've failed, how much pain I've felt and how I've begun learning from God but have so much more to receive before I can claim to be healed.'

But Keith was insistent that the brokenness I was feeling was integral to my ability to relate my story. Over the next few weeks I thought, prayed, planned and began writing. Whether or not the final product would be published was immaterial. The experience of writing, ordering my thoughts and analysing the events of the previous eight years was cathartic and central to my continuing healing. You are holding the finished product in your hands! During the writing of this book, however, I have been privileged to minister in many ways as a direct result of the ordering of my thoughts. While I have known the theology for many years, it has been an extraordinary experience to have God take my weakness and use it for his glory. It has been a real privilege to have him take my defeat and turn it into his victory. But that is the glory of the gospel. That is the actuality of discipleship.

DEEP GRACE

The conversation between Jesus and Peter recorded in John 21:15–19 is one of the most powerful episodes in scripture. There is an intense vulnerability shown by both partners that makes for an extraordinary climax to John's Gospel. There is much for us to learn from this passage that will encourage us to share our own story of grief in the sure knowledge that God can, and will, use us in our moment of absolute weakness.

Peter was a man of spiritual contradiction. He was intensely loyal to Jesus and was a most fervent disciple. Yet he was a man of frailty too and, at moments of crisis, he was prone to spiritual failure. I think it is easy to be too hard on Peter in this regard. The realization that one is walking on water, for instance, would be enough to make even the least scientific of us entertain doubts in our mind. Likewise, it would have been a strong man indeed not to be plagued by fear in the courtyard as Jesus was going through his trial. We can understand Peter denying a relationship with Jesus even if we would not wish to condone such a response.

However, these spiritual frailties were not the greatest problem that Peter faced. Such were his love and loyalty that he absolutely hated himself for letting Jesus down so badly. Peter was racked with guilt and was very hard on himself for his failures. This, of course, is a problem that so many of us face too. We may have spent many years faithfully serving the Lord and doing all we could to be obedient to his will. To be sure, we are all sinners and we have all fallen short of the glory of God, but many of us have done a reasonable job of discipleship. When we have been traumatized by the experience of bereavement and loss, however, our spiritual and emotional reactions may have been completely unpredictable and absolutely out of character. This has most certainly been the case with me. There are times when I have doubted. There are times when I have hated God and angrily railed against him. There have been moments when I believed that God was somehow testing me or, even worse, punishing me. If that were the case, then I was clearly failing the test or was deserving of the punishment. There have been times when I failed to pray or just could not be bothered to pray. There have been times when I have been too weary or too uninterested to read the scriptures.

Reflecting on these attitudes, I would become plagued by guilt and feel like the biggest hypocrite on the face of the planet. How could I let God down so badly? Feeling worthy only of condemnation, I would be even less inclined to spend time with God, and so the cycle of apathy would continue. I would find my spiritual life spiralling out of control and I would not know how to redeem matters. I felt like a failure. I felt utterly useless to God. How could he possibly use a disappointment like me?

Peter had returned, with the other six Galilean disciples, to their home area. Physically tired and emotionally exhausted by recent events in Jerusalem, they were seeking sanctuary in the familiar. A fishing trip on a sea they knew well could prove to be the thera-peutic experience they needed so much. They were confused, they were hurting and they felt completely vulnerable and alone. Peter, more than the rest, had reason to feel helpless. Jesus had entrusted so much to him. His Lord had shown so much belief in him, even suggesting that he was the rock on which the Church would be built. Yet, when the chips were down, Peter had failed to keep the faith. He had let Jesus down and, as a result, felt that his spiritual collapse must result in the forfeiting of all spiritual ministry, let alone spiritual leadership. But, in his wisdom, Jesus chose that moment to show faith in Peter once more and restore him. There are five issues to notice about this process of restoration.

First, both the Gospel writer and Jesus mark the solemnity of the occasion in verse 15: 'After they had eaten, Jesus said to Simon Peter, "Simon son of John, do you love me more than these others do?"' The Gospel writer uses Simon's full name—Simon Peter. Jesus calls him 'Simon son of John', as he had done when Peter confessed Jesus as the Christ (Matthew 16:17). The reader is left in no doubt that the conversation to follow will be both sober and serious. There was a reserved formality about this encounter be-tween Lord and disciple. So it is when Jesus restores us after we have fallen short in our discipleship, either through sin or human weakness. To be sure, our restoration is made within the context of love. Nevertheless, it is a serious business because the cost of restoration is enormous, both to Jesus and to the individual being restored. For Jesus, the cost of restoration was his life laid down. As we shall see, the same is demanded of the one being restored.

Second, in restoring Peter, Jesus sought to confront him with the nature and extent of his spiritual shortcoming. Jesus framed the question in such a way as to stir up a memory within Peter. Jesus asked him, 'Simon son of John, do you love me more than these others do?' At first reading, such an approach seems fairly tactless. Asking Peter to compare his love with that of the other disciples standing nearby would potentially lead to a most embarrassing situation. However, Jesus was taking Peter back to the night of his betrayal and something the fervent disciple had said during the Last Supper. There, Peter had confidently claimed that, 'I will never leave you, even though all the rest do!' (Mark 14:29). So it was Peter who had first initiated the idea of a comparative love and loyalty between himself and his companions. In the light of his subsequent behaviour, there was no small irony in Jesus' question to him beside Lake Tiberias. The irony would not have been lost on Peter, who was now forced to acknowledge the credibility gap between profession and performance.

In addition, Jesus asked Peter the question, 'Do you love me?' three times. This, of course, mirrors the threefold denial by Peter concerning a relationship with Jesus. In these two ways, Jesus was confronting Peter with the errors he had made that had led to his spiritual failure. Jesus was not prepared to brush these errors under the carpet as if they had never happened. He knew that full restoration could happen only if Peter faced up to the reality of his shortcoming. Likewise, we too must objectively face the issues that so often cause us to fall when we grieve. Are we tired? Are we angry? Are we feeling guilty? What is it that is preventing us from living out a joyful relationship with God in the midst of our bereavement? Ignoring the issues will not make them go away. We need to face them objectively and courageously and allow Jesus to speak into our pain if full restoration and reconciliation is to occur. It can be an agonizing process because we may be forced to accept things about ourselves that we would rather not acknowledge. It is, however, a necessary process.

Third, there is a subtle exchange of ideas interweaved through the phraseology of Jesus' questions and Peter's responses. This is evident through the use of the word 'love' within their conversation. The delicate beauty of the Greek language is so often lost in translation. Nowhere is this more apparent than in this particular passage, the nuance of which is obscured in the English text. There are a number of different words in Greek that can be translated as 'love'—all of which have distinct meanings. Given the way in which this Gospel writer took extraordinary care over words, phrases and sentences in his work, the manner in which two specific words for 'love' are used can surely be no accident.

The interchange revolves around the two Greek words *philo* and *agape*. The first of these speaks of a love that exists between people in an affectionate relationship. Three examples from scripture are: 'Those who love their father and mother more than me are not fit to be my disciples' (Matthew 10:37); 'If you belonged to the world, then the world would love you as its own' (John 15:19); and 'To the angel of the church in Philadelphia write…' (Revelation 3:7). The name of this city literally means 'brotherly love'.

The word *agape*, however, is often used to denote a different idea about love. There seems to be an intensity and a spirituality attached to this word that is not reflected in *philo*. Here are some examples from scripture: 'The Father loves his Son and has put everything in his power' (John 3:35); 'You love him, although you have not seen him' (1 Peter 1:8); and 'This is what love is: it is not that we have loved God, but that he loved us and sent his Son to be the means by which our sins are forgiven' (1 John 4:10).

So, the difference between *philo* and *agape* is subtle but is vital for the interpretation of the passage we are currently studying, for it is in the different words used that we are able to find such hope for restoration in our own broken lives.

In verse 15, Jesus asked Peter the question for the first time: 'Simon son of John, do you love me more than these others do?' The word Jesus used here is a derivative of *agape*, so he was asking Peter to affirm an intense sense of spiritual bonding between disciple and Master. Peter, however, was only too aware of his recent failures. He knew that his behaviour had revealed the truth—that he was spiritually weak and fallible. His reply to Jesus reflected that: '"Yes, Lord," he answered, "you know that I love you."' But the word he used was *philo*. It is as if Peter wanted to say, 'Yes, Lord, I do love you. But I can't love you the way in which you want me to.' This was a most amazing admission of frailty by a man who had spent the previous three years making great claims for his love, loyalty and intensity of discipleship. Jesus knew exactly what Peter was saying but rather than passing him over for someone else who could fulfil the role, Jesus simply replied, 'Take care of my lambs.'

In verse 16, the question is asked again: 'Simon son of John, do you love me?' Again, the word Jesus used is a derivative of *agape* and, again, Peter's affirmative reply used the word *philo*. There was to be no mistake as to the intention of both questioner and responder. To ask and reply in such terms only once may have been coincidental. The same pattern repeated a second time makes a serious point. Yet again, Jesus affirmed Peter in his weakness by asking him, 'Take care of my sheep.'

But something quite extraordinary happens in verse 17. This time, when Jesus asked the question, 'Simon son of John, do you love me?' there was a shift in meaning. Here, Jesus himself used the word *philo*. It is as if he was acknowledging Peter's frailty and commending him for the self-understanding that the disciple had now developed and then, in that context, asking him this: 'OK, Peter, you can't be the super-disciple you wanted to be. You can't be the hero you always thought you were. You are not as strong and self-reliant as you thought you were. So all I want you to do is just love me as best you can. Will you do that?' This, I believe, is the reason why the Gospel writer goes on to note that 'Peter was sad' (v. 17). His sadness was not born out of a belief that Jesus did not trust him. His sadness came from the realization that he was weak and vulnerable—just like everyone else. So he replied with a sense of resignation and maybe with a heavy heart, 'Lord, you know everything; you know that I love you!' Of course, the word he used is *philo*.

Finally, Peter and Jesus had found a level. Peter had admitted his failings, he had acknowledged his weakness and he had declared his inability to give anything other than his brokenness to Jesus. He wanted to give more but knew that he could not. The response of Jesus was to accept Peter's brokenness and say a final time, 'Take care of my sheep.' That was the ultimate statement of restoration.

Jesus was saying that even though Peter was a failure and could minister only out of a broken spirit, it would be enough. Indeed, more than just being enough, it was absolutely the perfect disposition out of which to begin building the Church!

The truth is that Jesus wants broken people to minister to a broken world. He does not wait for us to be healed and completely sorted out before commissioning us with the task of caring for others. Jesus wants us to acknowledge our pain and our fragility of spirit and use those as the tools of Kingdom ministry. A number of people have suggested to me that I should have waited a while before writing a book on grief—that I should have 'got my head straight a bit more' before reflecting on my story. But that completely misses the point of John 21:15–19. Jesus wants broken ministers—what Henri Nouwen termed 'wounded healers'—to be effective for him. The amazing truth is that God can take you *as you are now* and use you to stand with others who are hurting too. Your brokenness is not your greatest barrier to ministry. Your brokenness is your greatest tool in ministry. The impact of grief does not make mission impossible. It makes mission possible.

Fourth, we note from this passage the awesome nature of the calling on us to minister out of brokenness to others who are in pain. A short while ago, I was licensed as minister of a new parish. It was a beautiful service, packed with rich symbolism and deep meaning. At one stage, I knelt before my bishop and he handed the licence over to me, saying, 'Receive the cure of souls, which is both yours and mine.' I was struck by the extraordinary privilege and responsibility that was being entrusted to me by God—the cure of souls. There is a sense in which that is the ministry entrusted to all God's people—that we are to love one another, pray for one another and minister to one another. Each one of us is called to 'the cure of souls'. The immensity of this ministry would not have been lost on Peter as Jesus repeatedly asked him to feed and tend God's flock. Yet, in the strength and power of the Holy Spirit, Peter was able to fulfil that calling with supernatural success, as the Acts of the Apostles bears witness. There is an almost incomprehensible

God of the Valleysegment

promise made to us by Jesus in John 14:12: 'I am telling you the truth: those who believe in me will do what I do—yes, they will do even greater things, because I am going to the Father.' It is an awesome, incredible calling on each one of us to be ministers in the name of Christ. Yet our human frailty is no barrier to achieving great things in his name because we are empowered by his Holy Spirit.

Finally, we note from this passage not just the awesome nature of our calling but also the costly nature of our calling. The conversation between Jesus and Peter ended as it had begun—with an air of solemnity. Jesus declared to his disciple, 'When you are old, you will stretch out your hands and someone else will bind you and take you where you don't want to go' (v. 18). In the following verse, the writer of the Gospel interprets this as a prophetic reference to the subsequent crucifixion of Peter. Jesus was clearly stressing to Peter the sacrificial nature of the ministerial task he was being asked to undertake. While not many of us will be required to lay down our lives for Christ in such a horrific way, each one of us is asked to lay down our lives and become both sacrificial and vulnerable in our ministry to others. This is clearly evident if we seek to use our own pain as a tool for coming alongside others who grieve. In the process of offering pastoral support, much may be required of us. We will need to be honest about our failings and the many ways in which we have let God down on our own journey through bereavement. We may be required to talk about details in our life that we would rather leave in the silence of our memories. Most painful of all, we will undoubtedly be required to cry with others who are grieving and absorb their pain into our own hearts.

This encounter between Jesus and Peter recorded in John 21:15–19 is so powerful and speaks so deeply into the experience of those who grieve. There is a clear message of hope at the heart of the story. The hope we have is that, even in the midst of all our pain, confusion, heartache and turmoil, we are adequately resourced and equipped to do the work of God. It does not matter how much we may think we have failed him. It does not matter how weak we are or how tired we feel. It does not matter how

126

useless we may feel. Our weakness is our story; our frailty is our strength; our defeat is God's victory. We are called to undertake a most awesome task. We are asked by God to use our pain and our vulnerability to bring glory to his name. We are asked to look beyond ourselves and seek to serve others who are hurting. Why does he ask that of us? Because, in Jesus Christ, that is exactly what he has done for us.

In the love of Christ, healing and restoration are possible. In the strength of Christ, mission is possible. We are sent out in the power of the Holy Spirit and with the promise of Jesus to all who believe in him: 'I will be with you always, to the end of the age' (Matthew 28:20).

Let us go, equipped with the peace of Christ and the pain of personal experience, to love and serve the Lord. Amen.

TWO STORIES
OF REDEMPTION

Two weeks after Rebekah was born, Clare and I went to a friend's ordination service in Coventry Cathedral. It was a wonderful service of celebration and Coventry is home to the most exquisite cathedral. After the service was finished, we spent an hour or so walking around the buildings, enjoying the architecture and artwork. The new cathedral is set adjacent to the ruins of the old cathedral, which was completely devastated by the Luftwaffe on 14 November 1940. It is most remarkable for the fact that, under the ministry and vision of the Provost at the time, Dick Howard, the new cathedral would be dedicated to the ministry of peace and reconciliation. This was reflected in the design itself. For example, two of the charred roof timbers had fallen in the shape of a cross. These were placed on an altar created out of rubble under the words 'Father Forgive'. A local priest, Revd Arthur Wales, made another cross out of medieval nails. The new cathedral, however, is dominated by Graham Sutherland's extraordinary tapestry, *Christ in Glory*. Taking ten years to create, and measuring 23 metres by 12 metres, the tapestry weighs over a ton. Based on Revelation 4:2–7, it depicts Christ in a semi-sitting position on a throne surrounded by the four living creatures. Sutherland described his intention in portraying Christ as he did: 'The figure must look real—in the sense that it is not a rehash of the past. It must look vital, non-sentimental, non-ecclesiastical, of the moment, yet for all time.'[17]

As we stood in front of the tapestry, neither Clare nor I spoke. I am not particularly arty but Clare was very gifted in that regard and was often profoundly moved by artistic expression. That was most certainly the case on this occasion as tears filled her eyes. She pointed out to me the remarkable interpretation of Christ's face. Half of the face was beautiful and glorified; half of the face was charred and burnt. That, as she explained to me, was a perfect representation of glory—a mixture of beauty and pain. The risen Christ ascended to heaven and was glorified at the right hand of God. But, even now, he wears the marks of crucifixion and the scarred persona of one who has borne our pain so that we might know forgiveness, healing and reconciliation.

The message of Christ to us through that tapestry was that we too, as beloved children of God, are defined in equal proportions by glory and pain. The anguish of grief, the torturous pain of bereavement, scars us for life. But through the process of redemption and healing, the scarring that marks our mind, body and soul is matched by the curative therapy of the Holy Spirit. If we are to experience the glory that Christ longs to give, then we must learn to live with both the scars and the splendour. We must give both the scars and the splendour back to God so that he can use us to bring glory to his name and healing to others who hurt.

One month before Clare died, she suffered a major coronary attack and was rushed into the resuscitation unit of our local hospital. For the next ten days, she was moved between three hospitals, each one specializing in a different aspect of the care she needed at that moment. The third move was to a hospital that offered palliative care to cancer patients. It was the hospital where my sister had died some months previously. The seriousness of Clare's situation was not lost on us.

Clare was wheeled on to the ward and was gently helped on to her bed. As she made herself comfortable, we became aware of a couple on the bed opposite. The lady was a patient and she was sitting with her husband, absorbed in an argument. The argument intensified as the minutes passed and the lady began sobbing. Their conversation got louder and louder until the woman finally shouted at her husband.

'What do you mean, "you understand"? You don't understand at all! How can you or anybody understand? You have no idea what it feels like to be trapped inside this body. It's OK for you—you can go home in a minute and do whatever you want to do this evening. I haven't got any choice but to stay here, have I? That's the problem with this bloody illness—there are no choices. I have no choice about any of it!'

Clare had been listening to the conversation as she unpacked her toiletries. At that moment, she did something completely out of character. She turned to this woman she had never met and she intervened.

'Excuse me,' Clare said slowly and quietly. 'I couldn't help but hear what you just said. And I think you are wrong. You and I do have a choice. We are both going to die soon. We can either choose to die with dignity or die without dignity. It's tough on us both. But we do have a choice.'

I do not know what happened to that woman, but I do know that, a few weeks later, Clare died with great dignity—at peace with herself and strong in the faith of Christ. I do know that her comments to that woman laid the foundation for the manner in which I have tried to come to terms with my own loss. It has not been at all easy. There have been moments of anguish and pain, the intensity of which I would scarcely have believed possible. I am keenly aware that I still have a long way to go and much healing yet to receive from God. But I have tried, at all times, to remain dignified in grief.

There is, for all of us, a choice. We can either grieve with dignity or without dignity. I do not mean the kind of dignity that is expressed through keeping 'a stiff upper lip'. I mean the kind of dignity that God has bestowed upon us as his children. We are made in the image of God. We have received every blessing in the heavenly realm. We have been chosen for a purpose and each one of us has a ministry to fulfil. Through the deep grace and love of

God, we have dignity. We can either live out that destiny or go another way.

It may be tough, but we do have a choice. In the strength and power of God, the choice is ours.

NOTES

1   *The Cloud of Unknowing*, trans. Clifton Wolters, Penguin,
    1978, pp. 53f.
2   Walter Brueggemann, *Israel's Praise*, Fortress, 1994, p. 129.
3   *Israel's Praise*, p. 133.
4   Karl Barth, *Church Dogmatics*, ed. G.W. Bromiley and T.F.
    Torrance, tr. G.W. Bromiley, T&T Clark, 1956–57
5   R.B.Y. Scott, *The Way of Wisdom*, MacMillan, 1972
6   John Calvin, *Commentary on the Book of Psalms*, 1.357.
    Translated by James Anderson, 5 vols, printed for the Calvin
    Translation Society, MDCCCXLV
7   Joni Eareckson, *A Step Further*, Bantam, 1976
8   Sarah Doudney, 'The Hardest Time of All', *Psalms of Life*,
    Houlston, 1871
9   Walter Brueggemann, *Genesis: Interpretation*, Westminster
    John Knox Press, 1986
10 L. Madow, *Anger: How to Recognize and Cope With It*,
    Scribners, 1972
11 Karl Barth, *Church Dogmatics*, ed. G.W. Bromiley and T.F.
    Torrance, tr. G.W. Bromiley, T&T Clark, 1956–57, IV.1, p. 515
12 Dietrich Bonhoeffer, *The Cost of Discipleship*, 1949
13 William Temple, *Citizen and Churchman*, Eyre & Spottiswoode,
    1941, p. 74
14 Elisabeth Kubler-Ross, *On Death and Dying*, Simon and
    Schuster, reprinted 1997
15 Terry Waite, *Taken On Trust*, Doubleday, 1993
16 John Bunyan, *Prayer*, Banner of Truth, 1965, p. 33. (This
    sermon was first published as *A Discourse Touching Prayer*,
    1662.)
17 Cited in R. Berthoud, *Graham Sutherland: A Biography*,
    Olympic Marketing Corporation, 1982, p. 205

HOPE IN THE WILDERNESS

BIBLE READINGS FROM ADVENT TO EPIPHANY
DAVID WINTER

'The world has many stories. Some make us laugh, some make us cry, some we forget and others we remember all our lives. But there are a few, very few, that mirror the human experience so vividly and completely that they have themselves become part of that experience. This book retells and reflects on perhaps the greatest of them all, the Exodus—the story of a group of men and women, with a charismatic but flawed leader, making their way from slavery in Egypt to a promised land "flowing with milk and honey".

'It is also a story with profound meaning for many people at the personal level. I began this book while my wife was ill in hospital and completed it in the first year of a painful bereavement. For me it became the story of a slow and arduous journey through a barren and desolate landscape towards a place of distant promise.'

Follow the story with David Winter, in this book of Bible readings and comment for every day in the season of Advent and Christmas, and discover how we too, like the people of Israel long ago, live under the justice and mercy of God.

ISBN 1 84101 258 0   £6.99

Available from your local Christian bookshop or direct from BRF using the order form on page 141.

IN THE PALM OF GOD'S HAND

A DIARY OF LIVING AGAINST THE ODDS

WENDY BRAY

'Sharing a diary like this is about more than baring your soul. It's like taking your clothes off in public in mid-January and asking passers-by to throw snowballs at you. Not something you would do unless you hoped an awful lot of good would come of it. But here I am, doing it… Whatever good might result is God's to reveal. I would hope that it will involve glory to him and comfort and encouragement to others, as well as providing the occasional laugh.'

This prayer diary testifies how personal faith can transform the hardest of times, and how God's love and mercy still break through, no matter how tough the situation. Rob Parsons writes in the introduction: 'This is a book about trust. Not the kind of trust that says, "I know that soon it will be all right again", but rather the kind that trusts God—anyway—sometimes because there is just no-where else to go.'

ISBN 1 84101 336 6   £6.99

Available from your local Christian bookshop or direct from BRF using the order form on page 141.

OH GOD WHY?

A SPIRITUAL JOURNEY TOWARDS MEANING, WISDOM AND STRENGTH

GERARD W. HUGHES

The notion of a journey can be a helpful way of understanding the meaning of our own lives, our grumbles and discontents, our pain and sadness, our hopes and dreams. And seeing our lives as a journey with Christ to God, who loves us beyond our imagining, can transform the daily walk of faith beyond recognition.

Drawing inspiration from the Spiritual Exercises of Ignatius of Loyola, Gerard Hughes has written a book of Bible readings that help us to 'pray the Bible' in a unique way. It includes helpful introductory chapters on the importance of prayer, Bible study, and other spiritual disciplines, including keeping a 'faith journal', whether you can spare fifteen or even just two minutes a day. There is also a section of material for groups working through the book together.

ISBN 0 7459 3538 9 £7.99

Available from your local Christian bookshop or direct from BRF using the order form on page 141.

THE ROAD THROUGH THE DESERT

MAKING SENSE OF WILDERNESS TIMES

ALISON JACOBS

Feeling emotionally and spiritually dry? In some way defeated? Even despairing?

Many people—both Christians and non-believers—feel alienated not only from God but from the world in which they live, either through some kind of loss or difficulty, or simply because each day seems like one big struggle. This is no new problem! *The Road through the Desert* is a practical and thought-provoking guide which follows Moses and the Israelites on their Old Testament wilderness wanderings, drawing out lessons to help to bring today's 'wilderness travellers' into the Promised Land that God has ready for them.

Alison Jacobs is an accredited Methodist preacher, based in Lincoln. Since 1994 she has had ME, the chronic fatigue condition, which has contributed to her own wilderness experience.

ISBN 1 84101 138 X £5.99

Available from your local Christian bookshop or direct from BRF using the order form on page 141.

BEAUTY FROM ASHES

READINGS FOR TIMES OF LOSS
JENNIFER REES LARCOMBE

'When my life seemed burnt to ashes, the last thing I could cope with was reading lengthy Bible passages, yet the Bible contains many verses which encourage and comfort people who are grappling with grief and loss. I began collecting these verses and sticking them all over my kitchen walls! My favourite verse reminded me that God could transform the ashes of my life into something new and beautiful. This book grew out of my collection of "kitchen verses", combined with some of the practical tips and helpful ideas for those adjusting to loss of various kinds, given to me at the time by others who know how it feels from personal experience.'

This is a book for keeping by the bedside, for dipping into just for a few moments every day, offering help along the way for the hardest of times.

ISBN 1 84101 124 X £5.99

Available from your local Christian bookshop or direct from BRF using the order form on page 141.

PRAYING THE JESUS PRAYER
TOGETHER

BROTHER RAMON & SIMON BARRINGTON-WARD

The Jesus Prayer is an ancient yet simple form of contemplative prayer, rooted in scripture. Over the last few decades it has spread out of the Eastern Orthodox tradition and into the lives and spirituality of Western Christians, causing a quiet revolution.

Both Brother Ramon (the hermit) and Simon Barrington-Ward (the bishop) had been practising and teaching the Jesus Prayer for well over twenty years when they came together for a shared week of prayer at Glasshampton Monastery. This book shares what they learned in an experience they described as a 'week of glory', yet also marked by the physical suffering of Brother Ramon's illness.

ISBN 1 84101 147 9   £6.99

Available from your local Christian bookshop or direct from BRF using the order form on page 141.

TO HAVE AND TO HOLD

BIBLE STORIES OF LOVE, LOSS AND RESTORATION

ANNE JORDAN HOAD

These imaginative retellings of Bible stories, some familiar, some less well-known, bring to life characters who, like so many of us, struggle in their personal relationships. It is easy to idealize such characters, assuming that they were somehow superior to mere human beings —and in idealizing them, we miss out on the lessons we can learn from their all-too-familiar experiences. Like us, they had to confront complex choices, survive difficult circumstances, wrestle with jealousy, dishonesty and pride. In hearing their stories again, we can identify and share in their fears and hopes, their sorrows and joys.

ISBN 1 84101 036 7   £6.99

Available from your local Christian bookshop or direct from BRF using the order form on page 141.

ORDER FORM

REF	TITLE	PRICE	QTY	TOTAL
258 0	*Hope in the Wilderness*	£6.99		
336 6	*In the Palm of God's Hand*	£6.99		
3538 9	*Oh God Why?*	£7.99		
138 X	*The Road through the Desert*	£5.99		
124 X	*Beauty from Ashes*	£5.99		
147 9	*Praying the Jesus Prayer Together*	£6.99		
036 7	*To Have and to Hold*	£6.99		

POSTAGE AND PACKING CHARGES						
order value	UK	Europe	Surface	Air Mail	Postage and packing:	
£7.00 & under	£1.25	£3.00	£3.50	£5.50	Donation:	
£7.01–£30.00	£2.25	£5.50	£6.50	£10.00	Total enclosed:	
Over £30.00	free	prices on request				

Name _____ Account Number _____

Address_____

_____ Postcode _____

Telephone Number _____ Email _____

Payment by: Cheque ❑ Mastercard ❑ Visa ❑ Postal Order ❑ Switch ❑

Credit card no. ❑❑❑❑ ❑❑❑❑ ❑❑❑❑ ❑❑❑❑ Expires ❑❑ ❑❑

Switch card no. ❑❑❑❑❑❑❑❑❑❑❑❑❑❑❑❑❑❑

Issue no. of Switch card ❑❑❑❑ Expires ❑❑ ❑❑

Signature _____ Date _____

All orders must be accompanied by the appropriate payment.

Please send your completed order form to:
BRF, First Floor, Elsfield Hall, 15–17 Elsfield Way, Oxford OX2 8FG
Tel. 01865 319700 / Fax. 01865 319701 Email: enquiries@brf.org.uk

❑ Please send me further information about BRF publications.

Available from your local Christian bookshop.   **BRF is a Registered Charity**

New Daylight, BRF's popular series of Bible reading notes, is ideal for those looking for a fresh, devotional approach to reading and understanding the Bible. Each issue covers four months of daily Bible reading and reflection with each day offering a Bible passage (text included), helpful comment and a prayer or thought for the day ahead.

New Daylight is written by a gifted team of contributors including Adrian Plass, Margaret Cundiff, David Winter, Rob Gillion, Rachel Boulding, Peter Graves, Helen Julian CSF, David Spriggs, Jenny Robertson and Veronica Zundel.

New Daylight is also available in large print and on cassette for the visually impaired.

NEW DAYLIGHT SUBSCRIPTIONS

❑ I would like to give a gift subscription
(please complete both name and address sections below)
❑ I would like to take out a subscription myself
(complete name and address details only once)

This completed coupon should be sent with appropriate payment to BRF. Alternatively, please write to us quoting your name, address, the subscription you would like for either yourself or a friend (with their name and address), the start date and credit card number, expiry date and signature if paying by credit card.

Gift subscription name _____

Gift subscription address _____

_____ Postcode _____

Please send to the above, beginning with the next January/May/September issue: (delete as applicable)

(please tick box)	UK	SURFACE	AIR MAIL
NEW DAYLIGHT	❑ £11.10	❑ £12.45	❑ £14.70
NEW DAYLIGHT 3-year sub	❑ £27.45		

Please complete the payment details below and send your coupon, with appropriate payment to: **BRF, First Floor, Elsfield Hall, 15–17 Elsfield Way, Oxford OX2 8FG**

Your name _____

Your address _____

_____ Postcode _____

Total enclosed £ _____ (cheques should be made payable to 'BRF')

Payment by cheque ❑ postal order ❑ Visa ❑ Mastercard ❑ Switch ❑

Card number: ☐☐☐☐☐☐☐☐☐☐☐☐☐☐☐☐☐☐☐

Expiry date of card: ☐☐☐☐ Issue number (Switch): ☐☐☐☐

Signature (essential if paying by credit/Switch card) _____

❑ Please do not send me further information about BRF publicaations.

NB: BRF notes are also available from your local Christian bookshop.   **BRF is a Registered Charity**

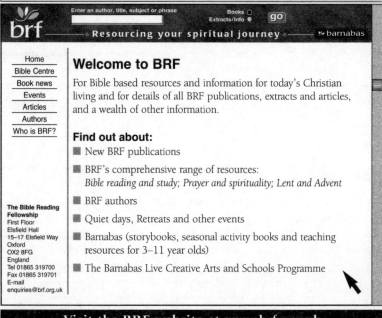

www.brf.org.uk

Enter an author, title, subject or phrase   Books ○
                                             Extracts/Info ●   **go**

brf ——— Resourcing your spiritual journey ——— ❧ barnabas

Home
Bible Centre
Book news
Events
Articles
Authors
Who is BRF?

**The Bible Reading
Fellowship**
First Floor
Elsfield Hall
15–17 Elsfield Way
Oxford
OX2 8FG
England
Tel 01865 319700
Fax 01865 319701
E-mail
enquiries@brf.org.uk

Welcome to BRF

For Bible based resources and information for today's Christian living and for details of all BRF publications, extracts and articles, and a wealth of other information.

Find out about:

■ New BRF publications

■ BRF's comprehensive range of resources:
Bible reading and study; Prayer and spirituality; Lent and Advent

■ BRF authors

■ Quiet days, Retreats and other events

■ Barnabas (storybooks, seasonal activity books and teaching resources for 3–11 year olds)

■ The Barnabas Live Creative Arts and Schools Programme

Visit the BRF website at www.brf.org.uk